Strategic Analysis

Routledge Research in Strategic Management

Strategic Analysis
Processes and Tools

Andrea Beretta Zanoni

Routledge
Taylor & Francis Group

LONDON AND NEW YORK

First published 2012
by Routledge

2 Park Square, Milton Park, Abingdon, Oxon OX14 4RN
711 Third Avenue, New York, NY 10017, USA

Routledge is an imprint of the Taylor & Francis Group, an informa business

First issued in paperback 2016

Typeset in Sabon by IBT Global.

Library of Congress Cataloging-in-Publication Data
Zanoni, Andrea.
 Strategic analysis : processes and tools / by Andrea Beretta Zanoni.
 p. cm.—(Routledge research in strategic management)
 Includes bibliographical references and index.
 1. Strategic planning. I. Title.
 HD30.28.Z36 2011
 658.4'012—dc22
 2011013349

ISBN: 978-0-415-88063-3 (hbk)
ISBN: 978-1-138-20309-9 (pbk)

Contents

Tables

Figures

x *Figures*

Introduction

The theme of strategic planning is of considerable current interest.

At its origins, in the early 1960s, strategy was interpreted as a general model for managing interactions between a firm and its environment (Chandler 1962, Andrews 1964, Ansoff 1965). However, given that in a market economy, the environment with which firms interact is competitive, very soon strategy took on a more precise meaning, identifying management activities concerned with managing competition.

By adapting a definition of biological origin, strategy can be defined as an interaction between agents characterized by constraints on resources and a low probability of individual goals being reached due to the presence and actions of other agents. Associating strategy with a phenomenon that, however fundamental, is nevertheless specific (competition) has a number of consequences.

First, the boundaries of strategic decisions are established, and the same is done for the techniques that can be used to take such decisions.

Second, strategic needs become variable, and, for firms, increase as competitive pressure increases.

This direct relation between competition and strategy explains why the importance of strategic planning has grown so significantly in recent years, and why it will presumably continue to grow in the near future. Research and field experience present a scenario in which competitive pressure continues to intensify. Economic crises and recession have accelerated and accentuated changes that were, to a certain extent at least, already underway. These changes relate in particular to:

- the competitive positioning of many firms;
- the configuration of global supply chains;
- the balance of alliances;
- the stability of raw materials markets;
- consumption propensities and habits;
- the pursuit of equilibrium between advanced and emerging economies;
- relations between different production technologies;
- conditions of access to capital.

The fact is that in a global arena in which everything from finance to the supply chain is so highly integrated, the barriers to competition that once protected firms, sectors and territories are becoming increasingly less restrictive and less resistant. Everything is more volatile: even competitive threats and opportunities are more frequent and less predictable, accentuating business risk. So-called sustainable competitive advantages are becoming increasingly rare and short-lived (D'Aveni et al. 2010).

A strategy may originate in many ways. However, to understand the framework underlying the strategy design process, it is helpful to refer to a firm's 'competitive structure', in other words a firm's strategic identity at every moment of its lifetime.

Competitive structure is a complex concept, in the sense that is determined by a range of factors:

- a firm's resources, or rather the combination of its resources, capabilities and strategic competences;
- a firm's technology and production portfolio;
- a firm's chosen positioning (one or more);
- the competitive configuration of company processes; in other words the way a firm organizes its activities to manage competition;
- the nature of the competitive spaces in which a firm is present (in turn, the outcome of the positioning choices of individual agents);
- for each competitive space, a firm's strengths and weakness in relation to the critical success factors of that space;
- for each competitive space, the resulting competitive positioning (advantage, disadvantage, equilibrium).

Competitive structures change over time. What causes them to change are decisions taken by the firm, the actions of competitors, government policies, technological innovations, etc. Strategic management of a firm means *manipulating changes in its competitive structure over time*, guiding it towards configurations that the firm's management considers desirable.

The process of planning and implementing a strategy, in other words the process of *manipulating* competitive structure, involves the following steps:

1. evaluation of the firm's current and future competitive structure (how it is now and how it may become in relation to certain assumptions);
2. modelling of a strategic design to achieve, with time, a given, desired competitive structure;
3. formalization of the strategic design in the form of a strategic plan as the final output of the planning process;
4. implementation of the plan accompanied by strategic control involving rolling updates.

The strategic design is thus the operating tool used to manipulate, to shape competitive structure over time. Strategic design requires specific analysis of strategic nature. Strategic analysis consists of the collection, collation and evaluation of data relevant to strategic decisions.

To facilitate the decision-making process, analysis should follow the same decision-making pathway from which strategic plans originate. Accordingly, in this book the process of analysis is presented in three phases: scenario analysis, competitive analysis and business impact analysis. Though the process of analysis makes use of certain logical tools (some quantitative) it should be seen as a learning process designed to foster rather than to stifle the creativity of the decision maker.

Performing strategic analysis does not involve adapting to clichés or prevailing ideas (if they still exist). On the contrary, analysis should be conducted specifically to avoid preconceptions and prejudice, to view reality from a different perspective.

A significant part of the literature now focuses on reducing the duration of competitive advantages (a shift from the concept of sustainable advantage to that of temporary advantage). This is the outcome of the increasing volatility of events that at times seems to frustrate all attempts at planning.

However, it is important to avoid erroneous assessments.

For some time now, one form of planning, that, for the sake of simplicity, can be defined 'extrapolative' planning, has been in crisis. The same is not true of strategic planning, that, on the contrary, in conditions of increasing competitive pressure, has become indispensable. Undoubtedly, strategic planning needs to be done in a different way to the past, with more focused, more intelligent, more rapid analysis, using planning methods that are more flexible and more responsive to strategic control, more oriented towards lifelong learning, and so on. Nevertheless, in firms, particularly medium-sized firms, strategic planning has a strange destiny: it's often spoken about, frequently out of context, yet at the same time it is seen as a residual activity, worthy of lip service but no action. This is a mistake, because the existence of a strategic plan considerably increases a firm's chances of exploiting competitive opportunities and reducing associated risks.

Finally, a debt of gratitude is due to Silvia Vernizzi and Giulia Solinas, of the Competitive Business Strategy Research Group (www.gdrstrategia. com/en), who wrote Chapters Two and Three and contributed to the development of many of the ideas presented in this work.

Milano, February 8, 2010

1 Planning Strategy

STRATEGY AND COMPETITION

In its earliest applications to the firm, the concept of strategy identified activities directed towards the management of relations with the external environment (Chandler 1962): for example, Ansoff distinguished very clearly between the strategic issues supposedly pertaining to external management, from the administrative and operational issues limited to the sphere of internal management (Ansoff 1965).

Everyone may have his or her own idea of what is meant by internal and external. And in fact, as early as the 1960s, at the extremes two perspectives were adopted: the broader, holistic, 'Harvard' approach that, following the Business Policy tradition, led to a vision of strategy as management of the whole; and the narrower, more technical strategic management approach that focused essentially on the external management of product/marketing mix choices.

In the present context, managing the relation that links a firm with its external environment essentially implies choosing how to face up to competition. By adapting to the social realm a concept of biological origin, competition can be defined as an interaction between parties in which:

- there are significant constraints on the availability of resources;
- the probability of each competitor achieving his or her goals is reduced by the presence and the actions of the others.

Forms of competition may be very diverse: individuals may compete to reach a certain ranking, or to survive on a desert island, together with, or to the detriment of, others.

Nevertheless, it is competitive constraints (resource limitations and the actions of others) that make it necessary to think and act strategically.

Competition has a number of intrinsic effects on the characteristics of strategic decisions, such as complexity, relevance or high risk of error. Note, however, that these are effects rather than constituent elements of the concept of strategy, and hence may characterize non-strategic decisions also.

For firms, competition is physiological; it is an institutional condition of free markets, one codified by rules and embedded in the customs of economic agents. Firms compete to win a share of the market for their products and services, to remunerate capital invested at least at the market rate (for the purchase of capital firms compete in a similar fashion).

In a free market, the necessary condition for equilibrium to be reached is the production of goods whose value to purchasers is higher than the value of the resources employed in their production (the value of all resources, including risk capital), i.e., when revenues are at least equal to costs ($R \geq C$).

All of this comes about through the workings of competition, in other words, it is an institutionalized contest between buyers, who might be considered 'territories' that firms discover and dispute among themselves over time. In other words, to ensure the condition ($R \geq C$), firms must win over an adequate share of buyers (R) in relation to resources consumed (C).

It is in this dimension that strategy in the sense of management of competition takes shape more clearly. The formulation of a business strategy implies deciding how to win over and maintain a share of buyers to ensure that the ratio of R to C is at least equal to one (or is reasonably likely to reach such a ratio). To conclude, in strictly operational terms it can be asserted that competitive goals include:

- maintaining existing buyers, or limiting their loss to an acceptable level (measured as the ratio of R to C);
- alternatively, winning over new buyers, consistent with the R/C constraint.

COMPETITIVE STRUCTURE

At each moment in its lifetime, a firm is in a certain state of competition, in other words, it adopts a given strategic posture or identity, regardless of whether its management is aware of such a state or posture.

This state or posture can be defined 'competitive structure' at time t_0. Competitive structure is a hybrid concept, in the sense that its component elements belong to non-homogeneous logical categories. In fact, competitive structure reproduces a frequently used relation, that between resources, choices and outcomes: borrowing a paradigm from industrial economics, it can be asserted that competitive structure is, at individual firm level, a specific combination of resources-conduct-performance (Figure 1.1).

The next step is to examine more closely the components of a competitive structure, departing from choices.

1. In terms of resources, we can distinguish between the stock of resources available to a firm, a firm's capability in deploying such resources, and the strategic competences that emerge from the interaction of resources and capabilities.

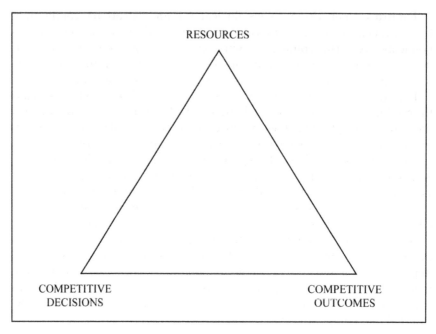

Figure 1.1   Competitive structure at time t_0.

2. The competitive state of a firm depends, then, on three fundamental choices relating to how the firm configures its technology portfolio (the set of processes and products a firm is able to manage and make), defines its competitive position and selects the competitive configuration of its business processes.
3. In terms of performance, competitive structure is composed of the competitive spaces a firm occupies (competitive spaces are a result, being dependent on the relative positioning of other firms), the factors critical for success in the competitive spaces, upon which a firm's strengths and weaknesses depend, and finally a firm's positioning in each competitive arena.

Overall, the elements of competitive structure are presented together in Figure 1.2.

Temporal dynamics are crucial to an understanding of the nature of competitive structure. At instant t_0 when a snapshot of competitive structure is taken, choices have not yet given rise to their expected outcomes and largely depend on resources accumulated in the past (resources that will change as a result of the aforesaid choices); it can also be seen that competitive performance depends on choices made some time before, as well as on the current state of strategic competences.

More in general, competitive structure is symptomatic of the complexity that characterizes all economic systems, business systems included. This complexity accounts also for the difficulty and uncertainty inherent in

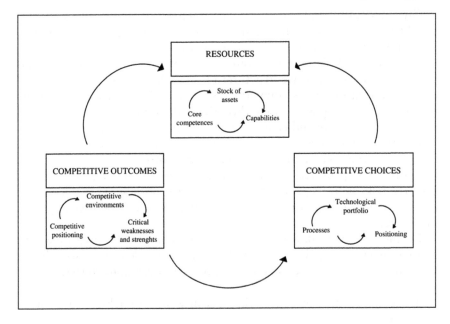

Figure 1.2   The elements of competitive structure.

forecasting the system's input-output relation. At times, the latter relation is difficult to reconstruct even ex-post, given that links between variables are casually ambiguous (this phenomenon will be examined more closely in due course) and the actions of exogenous variables are key determinants of the outcome of systemic activity.

Competitive structure changes over time, at a rate that naturally varies from situation to situation. The complex nature of competitive structure often makes transformations difficult to interpret. Nevertheless, competitive structures change continuously and a snapshot taken even a few moments earlier portrays a state that has already ceased to exist.

THE STRATEGIC DESIGN

The importance of competitive structure should be appreciated above all in terms of knowledge: for a firm, understanding the nature of competitive structure requires an in-depth assessment of its own competitive identity and of how this has taken shape over time. It has been seen, however, that competitive structures change. What changes competitive structures are the decisions a firm takes or fails to take, the activities of competitors, government policies, technological innovations and many other factors.

Strategic management of a firm implies management of its competitive structure, in other words, orienting its competitive structure towards configurations considered desirable or at least acceptable.

Given its nature and complexity, management of competitive structure should be achieved by means of a specific project or 'design', in other words, a set of decisions or actions planned in the future.

The strategic design is the operating instrument used to manipulate and shape over time competitive structure: a firm with no strategy fails to guide the transformation of its competitive structure. The essence of strategic design and planning is precisely this: giving direction to the dynamics of competitive structure and being able to control it over time.

Rejection of strategic management does not necessarily imply failure. Intuitions, other managerial competences and entrepreneurial capabilities have often compensated for an absence of strategic management. However, the risks increase, and at the same time the probability of adequately intercepting and exploiting to one's advantage new competitive opportunities decreases.

Because a strategic design must create a new competitive structure within a given time horizon, identification of its constituent elements is straightforward. In fact, a strategic design is basically a set of decisions concerning:

1. the competitive objectives that a firm wishes to achieve in a future period;
2. the strategic choices through which these competitive objectives will be achieved;
3. a set of planned actions that make it possible to implement strategic choices and achieve objectives;
4. the economic, financial and balance sheet impacts of strategic choices and planned actions.

Finally, it may be useful to recall the following characteristics of strategic management in a firm.

1. Strategy has a pervasive impact on management and organization, because it conditions, or should condition, the conduct of all business activities.
2. A firm's strategic needs are not constant and unchanging; on the contrary, they vary in relation to the intensity of the competition a firm faces. As competition intensifies, so, too, does the need for strategy, and hence the need to devise a strategic plan to achieve strategic goals. In turn, the intensity of competition is determined by environmental variables in both quantitative (number of competitors, geographical extent of competition, etc.) and qualitative terms (technological complexity, speed of change, etc.).
3. As strategic needs increase, strategic capabilities should increase also, in terms of specific competences in the drafting and implementation of strategic design (conceptually no different from the competences required to manage a firm's finance, business control or HR functions).

HOW IS A STRATEGIC DESIGN DEVISED? A FIRST RESPONSE: 'STANDARD' STRATEGIES

Having clarified the meaning of strategy, the next step is to explore how a firm can (or should) devise a strategy.

Initially, the pioneers of business strategy (managers, consultants, academia), in an attempt to simplify strategic management, made widespread use of 'standard' strategies, in other words, standardized responses coherent with given environmental dynamics. On a logical plane, the process of strategic elaboration was formulated in three consecutive phases (Kay 1993).

1. The initial phase involves evaluation of the environment in which a firm operates or intends to operate. From a more technical perspective, this phase derives directly from experience of budgeting and evolves progressively towards a number of evaluation systems, some sophisticated, such as scenario analysis (with extensive use of IT tools), others quantitative, such as the product life cycle model.
2. In the second phase, the firm formulates a strategy. The link with the first phase, i.e., with environmental assessment, is direct and immediate. To simplify the process, at this phase standard behavior models are identified.
3. In the third and final phase, strategy is implemented, from a perspective that, at least conceptually, resembles the cause-effect relation of Chandler's strategy-structure.

Examples of standard strategies abound: the four development strategies identified by Chandler, Ansoff's four vectors, or the strategic archetypes of Miles and Snow (defenders, hunters, analysts, reactors), the strategic matrices (BCG matrix, McKinsey matrix, A. D. Little matrix, etc.) with the standard forms of strategic behavior, such as defending or exploiting positions of strength, overcoming positions of weakness or abandoning the market.

Box 1 'Strategic archetypes' presents an in-depth analysis of the origins and development of standard strategies.

The appeal of the standard behavioral models, or of standard strategies, has always been remarkable.

In recent years, however, the propensity of academics and practitioners to formulate standard behavior models has diminished significantly. There may be a number of explanations for this. In particular, standard strategies imply classification of environmental states. The growing complexity of these days is little suited to be cataloged into states that, no matter how sophisticated, nevertheless remain predefined.

The approach pursued in this book is based not on standard behavioral models but rather on a process of analysis to support management in devising its own strategic plan.

STRATEGIC ANALYSIS AND DEVELOPMENT

Developing a strategic project is an arduous task, and implementing a strategic project is, as a rule, harder still. This book is concerned with developing a strategic project, and focuses on the process of analysis that should underlie decision making.

Strategic analysis can be defined as the collection, elaboration and assessment of data relevant to strategic decisions. Analysis is not an alternative to strategic creativity; it is a tool that serves to optimize the creativity of the decision maker and to reduce risks deriving from scarcity of information or methodological disorder.

The analytical process accompanies the decision-making process within the strategic project. As we have seen, there are four decision classes (objectives, strategies, actions and economic and financial implications). From the process perspective, these four decision classes translate into the following choices (Figure 1.3).

- Choices relating to competitive positioning, compatible with the production technology available (or achievable within a given time horizon).
- Choices relating to possible changes in the production portfolio, i.e., the development or acquisition of new production technologies or sale of current technology.
- Choices relating to competitive objectives for each positioning.
- Choices relating to the competitive design of business processes.

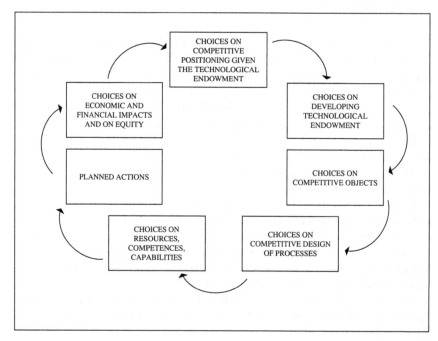

Figure 1.3   The choices in the strategic project.

- Choices relating to the configuration of resources, capabilities and strategic competences.
- Choices relating to planned actions.
- Choices relating to economic and financial outcomes.

Each choice clearly relates to traditional levels of strategy, expressed in terms of corporate, business and functional strategies. In fact, in general terms:

1. decisions relating to competitive positioning (objectives and positioning choices) belong to the realm of business strategy;
2. decisions relating to the production portfolio, resources, capabilities and competences belong to the realm of corporate strategy;
3. decisions relating to the competitive configuration of processes, planned actions and their economic and financial outcomes depart from the functional level and come together at the corporate level.

In the process of developing a strategic design three distinct phases of analysis can be identified and defined. At level one, within the scenario analysis, we take into account:

- the 'embryonic' competitive vision;
- the internal coherence of current competitive structure;
- global scenarios;
- industry scenarios.

At level two, within the competitive analysis, we focus on the assessment of choices relating to:

- competitive positioning;
- competitive objectives;
- competitive configuration of processes and configuration of resources, capabilities and strategic competences.

Finally, at level three, within the impact analysis, we elaborate information relevant to:

- the definition of planned actions;
- the assessment of economic and financial impacts;
- the implementation of the business plan, in the sense of formal output of the strategic project.

PLAN OF THE BOOK

This book is dedicated to exploring how to develop a process of strategic analysis to support the elaboration of a strategic design.

What has been said in these introductory pages makes it possible to outline the organization of the rest of the book. The remaining chapters are thus organized as follows:

- Chapter Two is concerned with the principal quantitative tools for conducting strategic analysis;
- Chapter Three is focused on the qualitative tools of strategic analysis;
- Chapter Four examines the components of competitive structure, offering an in-depth analysis of their principal characteristics and of how they relate to one another;
- Chapter Five begins with the process of analysis, specifically scenario analysis, from embryonic competitive vision to verification of the internal coherence of current competitive structure, moving on to the general scenario and the industry scenario;
- Chapter Six focuses on competitive positioning, activities, resources, capabilities and competences;
- Chapter Seven, the final chapter, deals with planned actions, economic, financial and balance sheet outcomes, and on the business plan.

Box 1   'Strategic archetypes'

Giulia Solinas

Strategic Archetypes: The Origins

It is of primary worth to mention the meaning of 'strategic archetypes' or generic strategies.

The main theoretical background is typically 'game theory', according to which the essence of every type of strategic behavior is an interaction between two or more individuals whose intents are either cooperative or to hinder the other players' actions so as to gain a satisfactory level of output (i.e., the pay-offs). As a result, the key features of game theory relations are noted here:

- optimization: every player aims at playing optimally, so that he or she tends to act in a rational manner in performing his actions;
- strategic interdependence: each player's choice takes into account not just his own achievement but also the other players' relative success.

In sum, individuals want to succeed in relationships in order to achieve the highest level of pay-off. The deals are dynamic; otherwise, they are played in a one-shot game. Furthermore the transactions are affected by three essential elements, that is to say i) the temporal dimension; ii) the information set available for each agent; iii) the strategy, i.e., a rule that indicates to the players which action to choose at each point in time, given his information set. A strategy specifies how to play in every possible distinguishable circumstance in which the player can find himself (Varian 2002, Gibbons 1996).

Box 1 (continued)

According to 'game theory' literature a strategic archetype is a definite set of actions, which form an overall strategy. The main peculiarity of strategy is the competitiveness: the list of actions is subjected to maximizing the pay-off amount, which the ideal would be to get by a player for every combination of a potential list of actions; that is to say that in sequential interactions the agents are going to behave strategically, whether they take into account the other players' choices and all combinations of potential strategies for both agents or steer towards different pay-offs entirely.

Summing up, strategic archetypes are deeply involved with competitive behavior and strategy, i.e., a definite number of actions matched in a complete decision plan that specifies how a player will act in every possible distinguishable circumstance in which he might be called upon to move (Gibbons 1996). The strategic archetypes aim to frame standardized strategic behaviors, from whose strategic choices depend in order to obtain the best level of pay-off.

The previous features had been encompassed in Strategic Management studies, for analyzing the competitive nature of firms.

To make rational choices managers usually are encouraged to adopt best practices, which can be summarized through a set of structures that enable agents to develop and launch products, to cope with market selection, or to develop innovation and steer methods. Thus, process-knowledge of strategic activities and policies, as well as the contents of competitive strategies, need to be formally identified. By adopting strategic archetypes frameworks, scholars and practitioners seek to formalize this bundle of managerial choices, which allow firms to better perform in order to alter strategic posture over time to better fit with contingency dynamics.

Mansfield and Fourie (2004) more recently defined strategy as the reflection of managerial choices and tactical responses versus that of similar competitors to create sustainable competitive advantage. Zott and Amit (2008) connote strategy as a pattern of managerial actions, which picture how firms position themselves to gain and maintain competitive advantage. Thus, effective strategy implementation requires that management build a strategy-focused organization, allocate resources, establish politics and take care about employee and shareholders (Thompson and Strickland 2001). These attempts have been named as *'strategic archetypes'* (Galbraith and Schendel 1983) or *'generic strategies'*, and they permit to measure or classify the content of various strategies (Robinson and Pearce 1988).

In a very general meaning, we may assume 'strategic archetype' as standardized behavior, which occurs when firms tend to achieve their objectives in contingency conditions. In fact, the contingency logic determines that *if* some conditions happen in a determinate competitive space and time, *then* the economic actor, i.e., firm or entrepreneur or any kind of political institution affected by competition, would reasonably act according to a strategic archetype. Consequently, strategic archetypes may be seen as the interpretative models of reality, that is to say, they are the lenses that induce strategic behavior in each peculiar case. In other words, archetypes are *'a set of structure and systems that reflects a single interpretative scheme'* (Greenwood and Hinigs 1993: 1052, reported in Brock 2006).

Box 1   (continued)

Table 1.1   Game Theory and Strategic Management: A Comparison

	Game Theory	Strategic Management
Strategy	It is a rule that indicates to the players which action to choose at each point in time, given his information set. A strategy specifies how to play in every possible distinguishable circumstance in which the player can find himself.	It is a pattern of managerial actions that explains how a firm achieves and maintains competitive advantage through positioning in relevant markets and dynamic environments.
Strategic Archetypes	It is a definite set of actions, which form overall a strategy.	Archetypes are a set of structure and systems that reflects a single interpretative scheme.

The Map of the Strategic Archetypes

The number of possible generic strategies, and their characteristics, may vary widely from author to author, so that the development of archetypal frameworks regarding strategic management is not homogeneous, but depends on the objectives of the firms as interpreted by each scholar (Galbraith and Schendel 1988). This is the first reason why it is not easy finding a unique approach to map them: because scholars want to sketch just a peculiar set of behaviors, it is hard to pull them towards general framework examples. In addition, the archetypal statement is often due to double order conditions:

- the existing ground theory;
- the empirical conditions that impact on the competitive firms' environment.

The first condition impacts the knowledge background of scholars who provide strategic archetypes, while the second one pictures the contingent environment that influence the competitive game among firms and triggers the operative logic, which stands at the cornerstone of any strategic archetype.

We may recognize two dimensions in order to map the main theoretical contributions. The first dimension concerns the firm's positioning gained with respect to relevant competitors as well as the overall environment. On the other hand, the second pillar pays attention to the intentions pursued by the firm, which can be simplified in two features: growing intent and optimizing intent.

The table below represents the cross of the relevant pillars. The blending features enclose archetypal families that can be labeled as *optimization-market archetypes, optimization-environment archetypes, dynamical growth-market archetypes* and *dynamical growth environment archetypes* (Figure 1.4).

Box 1 (continued)

The first dimension is concerned with the leading questions that inspired scholars and practitioners in developing standardized behaviors. In fact, the strategic standardized behaviors try to answer at least two general questions:

- how should a firm position itself in order to fit with the environment?
- how should a firm position itself among its rivals in order to achieve its goals, match with market needs and obtain positive returns?

In order to map strategic archetypes, we also may move towards another relevant question, which drives firms in selecting a path of competitive choices. Managers ask how to optimally arrange the organization to jointly determine a satisfactory level of performances and the firm's growth. That question broadly considers both the previous aspects, i.e., firm-performance relationship and firm-environment adaptation. For a rational firm, the behavior consists of optimizing the systemic structure and networks as a whole, both with reference to the environment and markets. These sets of actions are kept up in order for efficiency, productivity and gaining internal and external (holistic) equilibrium. Second, firms grow to survive (Penrose 1959), so that they must be able to set a dynamic path that induces them to grasp opportunities that permit obtaining a better position or more suitable environmental fitness. Summing up, the second pillar can be split into two sub-dimensions: 'optimization' and 'dynamical growth'.

The match of the two dimensions produces four categories of generic strategies. Miles and Snow (1978) identified four types, or generic strategies, that could be labeled as 'optimization environment archetypes', because they are applied in order to achieve successful alignment with the perceived environmental conditions. The four generic strategies are defined as 'defenders', 'prospectors', 'analyzers' and 'reactors'. Defenders

	GAIN MONEY Firm - market	WHO WE ARE Firm - environment
OPTIMIZE	OPTIMIZATION MARKET ARCHETYPES	OPTIMIZATION ENVIRONMENT ARCHETYPES
DYNAMICAL GROWTH	DYNAMICAL GROWTH MARKET ARCHETYPES	DYNAMICAL GROWTH ENVIRONMENT ARCHETYPES

Figure 1.4 Strategic archetypes: a map framing.

Box 1   (continued)

are firms with narrow product-market domains and they devote primary attention to improve the efficiency of their existing operations. Prospectors are organizations that continually search for market opportunity and have strong intentions to innovate. Analyzers operate both in stable and unstable product-markets, gathering innovative ideas and adopting them where they appear most promising. Reactors are firms that advance continuously environmental turbulences. Utterback's and Abernathy's (1975) work provides an example for the 'optimization market archetypes'. They selected three generic strategies:

1. 'performance maximizing', which emphasizes the product and/or service performance;
2. 'sale maximizing', which stresses marketing politics to increase total sales and market share of firm;
3. 'cost minimizing', which points up processes on technology and R&D to decrease total cost of production.

On the other side, Hofer and Schendel (1978) contribute with a model for the dynamical growth market archetypes. They formulate six generic strategies:

1. 'share increasing', where firms pursue high investments to increase market share;
2. 'growth' implies maintaining positions in the expanding market by implementing investment at industry norms;
3. 'profit' requires controlling costs to throw off cash;
4. 'market concentration and asset reduction', where firms realign resources to more focused and smaller segments;
5. 'turnaround' if the improvement of strategic posture may require investment;
6. 'liquidation' when managers generate cash while withdrawing from the market.

Finally, Changanti (1982) represents a framework of dynamical growth environment archetypes based on the relationship among growing industry, production rate, pricing and patenting.

Conclusions

It is worth mentioning that at the early stages of strategic thinking many scholars and practitioners hardly cooperated in developing a common awareness on strategic archetypes, thus standardized behaviors that a generic firm applies in a specific case of competition were a central item. Moreover, the attention in theorizing strategic archetypes decreased since strategic thinking became more sophisticated and more devoted to theoretical improvement, thanks to scholars belonging to Industrial Economics and later to the Resource-Based View approach. As a matter of fact,

Box 1   (continued)

the proportion of strategic types may vary with environmental dynamism (Gimenez 2000). The unstable nature of environments and markets complicates the definition of long-standing strategic behavioral paradigms. The traditional archetypal standards might have undergone a process of de-legitimization due to the forces for change. The turnover of the set of strategic behaviors could lead to the emergence of a new and substantially different archetypal framework. Besides, recent studies, e.g., Galan and Sanchez-Bueno (2009), suggest the continuing validity of the strategy-structure nexus and the challenging dynamical discovery of the theoretical resistance of the former strategic archetypes. Scholars and managers are both called for testing the actual relevance of generic strategies in a dynamic and fast-moving environment, because the previous approaches may no longer be viable with the actual problem of managing diversity and discontinuity in higher uncertain contexts, where new organizational forms, such as networks, may render the archetypal stream obsolete.

2 Quantitative Tools of Strategic Analysis

Giulia Solinas and Silvia Vernizzi

The tools of strategic analysis have always played a significant role in strategic theory and in strategic analysis in particular. Nevertheless, what is apparently missing in the literature is a classification or formalization that provides a ranking or mapping of the tools available to the strategic analyst.

Consequently, the purpose of this chapter and of the next one is to propose a classification of the tools of strategic analysis, to present a snapshot of the instruments available to the analyst and to describe their use within the complex process of analysis.

Notably, this chapter, after having briefly described the methodology and the technique for the classification of tools, will be focused on the quantitative instruments, whereas the following chapter will address the description of the qualitative instruments.

This chapter is structured in two parts:

1. the first one is focused on the description of the methodology and techniques for the classification of the tools;
2. the second one, is focused on the description of the tools based on a quantitative methodology.

METHODOLOGY AND DESCRIPTION FOR THE CLASSIFICATION OF TOOLS

Strategic analysis is a dynamic process that, by means of appropriate quantitative and logic-qualitative tools, provides insight into the competitive context in which a firm operates and the characteristics of a firm's resources.

The process of strategic analysis is thus a rational and technical process that, through use of specific analytical tools, allows critical variables (internal and external to the firm) to be assessed and assumptions to be made in relation to the possible future evolution of each element of analysis and the 'what if' that may result as a consequence.

In such a process, analytical tools are of prime importance. Indeed, they are the means, the instrumentation with which analysis is performed. These tools make it possible to examine critical variables, to process the information flow supporting critical assumptions and to arrive at conclusions that shape choices, decisions and hence lines of action.

A range of different tools may be employed in the process of analysis, depending on the nature of the information and the objectives of the analysis.

Analytical tools constitute the 'toolbox' the analyst opens up to conduct his assessment.

Given the multitude of problems to tackle in strategic analysis process, the choice of technical instrumentation is the outcome of a wide range of factors that the analyst must weigh up carefully.

In selecting his tools, the analyst makes a preliminary choice of method and explanatory language to use in processing the flow of information.

Depending on the overall objective of the analysis and the information base available, the analyst may opt either for a quantitative approach, which delivers numerical data as the final research outcome, or for a qualitative approach, which focuses on descriptive aspects. The choice of tools used to perform the analysis represents the final step in a reasoned decision-making framework; by this stage, the fundamental paradigms of research, methodology and techniques of inquiry have already been established.

'Methodology' refers to the study of method and reality; it is the part of the logic of inquiry concerned with rules, methodical principles and formal conditions underlying scientific research. Research methodology varies according to how knowledge is acquired; consequently, it is related to the researcher's perception of reality.

'Techniques', on the other hand, are specific operating procedures that follow the logical and methodological framework that has been defined. Techniques, thanks to the tools employed in processing the knowledge base and in describing the phenomenon under investigation, enable knowledge to be conveyed through learning. A logical continuum can be perceived between technical-instrumental aspects and methodology, though note the two are ontologically distinct, each of equal dignity and importance.

Without entering into the details of the various scientific paradigms, the nature and methodology of research can be subdivided into:

- quantitative methodology, based on the collection and analysis of data;
- qualitative methodology, based on interviews, case studies and conversations with the subjects involved in the investigation.

Strategic analysis cannot be wholly and exclusively identified with one or other methodology, but rather draws on the characteristic features of both, effectively being a synthesis of qualitative and quantitative methodological contributions.

Aspects of both methodologies thus ensure an appropriate degree of flexibility, a good 'fit' to the case study, a broad range of technical instrumentation to use as needed, and a productive complementarity between quantitative and qualitative research (Bresser-Pereira 2009, Lee and Hubona 2009).

In the light of these methodological distinctions, the tools of strategic analysis can be divided into two macro classes:

1. quantitative instruments using a methodology based on variables analysis and quantitative techniques involving mathematical modelling of the phenomenon under investigation;
2. qualitative instruments seeking to describe analytically the objects and phenomena under investigation through qualitative research.

As mentioned above, this chapter will primarily deal with the first kind of tools, the quantitative ones, leaving at the following chapter the description of the second kind of instruments.

Taking this logic a step further, one possible—though incomplete—reclassification of quantitative tools might result in the identification of the following groupings:

- tools based on the identification of indices
- tools based on the identification of means
- tools based on the study of variability and mutability (mean squared error, variance)
- tools based on the analysis of the relation between two variables (correlation, regression)
- tools based on logic-deductive analysis
- tools based on the processes of capitalization and actualization

TOOLS BASED ON THE IDENTIFICATION OF INDICES

Statistics is the discipline that studies methods for examining the phenomena of nature.

The fields of application of statistics are numerous, relating to all contexts in which decisions are based on the analysis of selected phenomena. Among such contexts is strategic analysis.

Within the discipline of statistics, it is the contribution of descriptive statistics that is of particular relevance to this chapter. Descriptive statistics is concerned with summarizing with appropriate measures the most significant characteristics of the phenomena under investigation.

The purpose of this section is to analyze some of the statistical methods most commonly used in the processes of strategic analysis underlining how these methods can become effective tools of strategic analysis.

The analysis of indices satisfies the need to identify summary measures that can be expressed numerically and enable, for example, benchmark comparisons or diachronic analysis based on temporal trends.

The process of summarizing data through analysis of indices substantially consists of anchoring a phenomenon to a representative unit of analysis. This act of association defines the variables whose relations and interdependencies will be studied.

A variable may require more than one indicator to be fully described; furthermore, one indicator may be related to more than one concept at the same time. The selection of which indicator to use to express a given variable is the result of an arbitrary choice made by the researcher that needs to be justified through a series of logical steps.

First, it is essential to make explicit in the design of inquiry the theoretical background of the issue to ensure appropriate definition of the paradigm that subsequently guides the entire process of analysis.

For each conceptual dimension, the following elements must be identified expressly:

- the variables that describe the phenomenon;
- the indicators related to the variables;
- the indices. They are constructed only in the next stage, when the need for a quantitative synthesis of the various aspects under investigation calls for a homogenous space-time comparison of data.

In this sense, therefore, indicators summarize variables relating to the phenomenon under investigation, whereas indices are the mathematical-statistical result of the synthesis of indicators. Despite this distinction in the common language, indicators and indices are often used as synonymous.

Table 2.1 presents the logical steps necessary to describe, for example, the probability of survival of the firm.

Indices are expressed formally in the theory of statistics and defined as relations that enable comparisons to be made between heterogeneous magnitudes, bringing to light relative time series variations.

Various categories of index numbers exist:

- elementary index numbers
- synthetic index numbers
- composite index numbers
- symbol index numbers

Elementary index numbers derive from the relation between measures representing single elements that are real in time and space. Elementary index numbers may be fixed or mobile. For fixed index numbers, the denominator is constant over time. Mobile index numbers, on the other hand, are based on a relation between measures, whose denominator is not fixed over time but refers to the previous time period, thus concatenating variables over time.

Synthetic index numbers are used to define quantitative variations in time and space observed on a set of elements rather than a single element, for example, a basket of producer goods. Two examples are the consumer goods index and the producer goods index. To construct these indices, a sample must be defined. For example, to determine producer prices, it is

Table 2.1 The Probability of Survival of the Firm: Indicators and Indices

Item	Variable	Indicators	Indices
Survival of the firm	Equilibrium	Economic equilibrium	ROE ROI ROA
		Financial equilibrium	Current ratio Quick ratio Cash flow to debt ratio Free cash flow to operating cash ratio
	Market	Pioneering markets	Number of pioneering markets; Number of incumbents.
		Firm tenure in the market	Average life of firms in the market Firms' turnover
	Technology	Technological capabilities and discontinuities	Market innovation rate Industry innovation rate Percentage of incremental innovations Average investments in R&D Number of firm's patents compared to market average
	Industry	Industry profitability	Firms' ROI and ROE compared to industry average
	Economic growth	Country growth	GDP growth rate Inflation growth rate
		Industry growth	Industry growth rate compared to GDP
	Production	Production efficiency	Stock turn rate
	Customers	Level of satisfaction	Relative number of customers Relative number of loyal customers
		Value to buyer	Price to production cost ratio

Source: Our adaptation of Franco et. al. (2009): 'Swift and Smart: The Moderating Effects of Technological Capabilities on the Market Pioneering-firm', *Management Science* 55(11): 1853.

necessary first to estimate a set of goods for which price-quantity variations are relevant. The synthetic index that indicates variations in sample items is constructed in a number of steps: first, the elementary index numbers of selected goods are calculated; then a summary is obtained from a weighted average of the indices.

Composite index numbers are used to summarize heterogeneous measures. For example, if in the course of strategic analysis a summary estimate of industrial activity is required, measures might include prices and quantities of raw materials, number of hours worked, quantity of output and level of use of industrial plants: by considering conjointly these elements and weighting them appropriately, a composite index is obtained.

Symbol index numbers make it possible to summarize variables not directly related to each other but nonetheless relevant to the phenomenon under investigation. For example, the number of patents registered by entities of diverse legal and institutional status may be used as an indirect index of the productivity of an economy.

Often, in the process of strategic analysis, certain micro- and macro-economic indices take on particular importance. These indices can be classified on the basis of the following three attributes.

In relation to the business cycle, these indicators may be divided into:

- procyclic indicators: a procyclic economic indicator moves in the same direction as the business cycle. So if the economy is doing well, this number is usually increasing, whereas if the economy is in a recession phase, this indicator is decreasing. The Gross Domestic Indicator is an example of procyclic economic indicator;
- countercyclic indicators: a countercyclic economic indicator moves in the opposite direction to the economy. For example, the unemployment rate rises as the economy deteriorates, so it is a countercyclic economic indicator;
- acyclic indicators: an acyclic economic indicator has no relation to business cycle.

In relation to the ability of each indicator to signal the business cycle trend, economic indicators may be classified as:

- leading indicators: leading economic indicators change before the economy changes. Stock market returns are leading indicators, as the stock market usually begins to decline before the economy declines, and they improve before the economy begins to pull out of a recession. Leading economic indicators are the most important type for analysts as they help predict what the economy will be like in the future;
- lagged indicators: a lagged economic indicator is one that does not change direction until a few quarters after a turnaround in the economy. The unemployment rate is a lagged economic indicator, such as

unemployment tends to increase for two or three quarters after the
economy starts to improve;

- coincident indicators: a coincident economic indicator is one that
moves with the economy. The Gross Domestic Product is a coincident
indicator.

Finally, in relation to the frequency of statistical surveys, indices may be
instant, daily, weekly, monthly, quarterly, etc.

Among the micro-economic indices, the indices of relative profitability and riskiness are of particular importance. These indices that derive
from studies of accounting and finance are numerous. Notable examples
are return on investment (ROI), return on equity (ROE), market share,
contribution margin index, profitability index.

The index of the profitability of investment, known as ROI (Return on
Investment) in the literature, indicates the profitability of core business.
The index is based on the ratio between operating income and invested
capital (total balance sheet assets invested in core business).

$$ROI = \frac{R.O.}{C.I.} \times 100$$

ROE (Return on Equity) shows the profitability of risk capital (equity)
invested in the firm. It is a ratio indicating the ability of the firm to attract
equity. This index is significant when compared to the return on alternative
investments, because it sums up the opportunity cost of the contribution of
capital in a particular firm. The rate reflects the ratio of net operating profit
to total risk capital:

$$ROE = \frac{R.N.}{C.P.} \times 100$$

Market share expresses a firm's ability to capture and satisfy demand. This
indicator is based on the ratio of demand satisfied by an economic agent
to global market demand. The index is of particular interest in relation to
market penetration indices, used for simultaneous comparison of supply
and demand and to identify positions of relative leadership in satisfying a
given need in a specific market.

The contribution margin index makes it possible to capture, at the forecasting stage, the relation between production costs, sales volumes and
profit. This index is on the ratio of contribution margin to sales[1], and shows
the impact of a change in sales on production costs in percentage terms.
This index is generally used in internal analysis to assess the efficiency of
production sites and the profitability of business areas.

---

1. The contribution margin defines the level of turnover required to cover fixed
costs once variable costs have been deducted. If the contribution margin is
insufficient to cover fixed costs, a loss is recorded for the period (R. H. Gar-
rison and E. W. Noreen 2003).

$$MdC = \frac{MdC}{Sales}$$

The profitability index is generally used in strategic analysis to assess and rank investment projects. This index is based on the ratio of the current value of cash flows from investment and the actual cost of investment. This value of this relation lies in its ability to forecast the internal rate of return on investment and to assess the goodness of the project: the higher the rate of profitability, the more desirable in current terms the investment. The index is constructed using methods for estimating future flows; for in-depth treatment the reader should refer to the specialist literature.

In conclusion, indices are based on a relation between two or more homogeneous or heterogeneous variables. In the case of heterogeneous variables, various dimensions of analysis are aggregated to increase the complexity of the survey, thereby ensuring that it more closely reflects the multidimensional reality of the phenomenon under investigation.

In strategic analysis index numbers allow a significant quantity of data to be re-elaborated in order to arrive a summary measure that can be expressed in quantitative terms.

This aspect is fundamental for several reasons. First and foremost, it enables macro-economic competitive scenarios to be defined analytically and synthetically, by measuring the GDP growth trend, the inflation rate trend, and more generally, by studying fluctuations in the business cycle that affect the competitive performance of the firms in the study.

The analysis of indices also makes it possible to describe in quantitative terms key industry indicators, which are summarized by one indicator obtained through aggregation of indices. Take for example studies on industries' structure (McGahan and Porter 1997): the rate of profitability of capital, based on a series of concatenated indicators, may be compared with average industry ROE and ultimately with market share.

Indices may be exploited to assess competitive positioning in various market segments, and to identify marginal profit growth during a given time period.

Moreover, adopting an internal perspective, indices make it possible to describe asset configurations, for example, by measuring the efficiency of productive processes through the quantity-cost of production ratio, or cost efficiencies in the distribution network; indices are also useful in the internal assessment of resources, by identifying synergies in technology use by relating technological innovations to the number of products to which they are applied.

Finally, note that it is not possible to provide a comprehensive list of all the indices used in internal or external analysis, in view of the considerable flexibility of this particular mathematical-statistical methodology. The most important aspect of the analysis of indices is the correct identification of variables and the analytical potential of data obtained from the relation.

TOOLS BASED ON THE IDENTIFICATION OF MEANS

Among the descriptive statistical methods used in the process of strategic analysis, means are of special importance. Means are methods that substitute, through a process of synthesis, the distribution patterns of a given phenomenon with one representative measure.

Various types of mean exist that differ in terms of the arithmetic algorithm used to obtain them and the significance of the information they convey. The means most frequently used as tools of strategic analysis are:

- the arithmetic mean
- the truncated mean
- the geometric mean
- the harmonic mean
- the median
- the mode

The arithmetic mean is one of the descriptive statistical methods most frequently used in strategic analysis. The arithmetic mean M_a of a set of values x_1, x_2, $x_3...x_n$, is obtained by dividing the total sum of the values by the number N of observations:

$$M_a = \frac{x_1 + x_2 + ... + x_n}{N}$$

When observations have different frequencies, observations need to be weighted by their respective frequencies to arrive at the weighted arithmetic mean:

$$M_a = \frac{\sum_{i=1}^{r} x_i n_i}{N}$$

The significance of these relations is the same: the arithmetic mean indicates the share of the total due to each unit when the sum is divided into N equal parts.

The use of the arithmetic mean as a tool of strategic analysis is very frequent due to its ease of application on the one hand and to the immediacy of the information it provides on the other.

For example, the arithmetic mean could be correlated to the average share price trend, to average royalties accrued on trademark licenses, or to average revenues received or receivable in a given time period.

Despite the advantages of ease of application and immediacy of information, the arithmetic mean has a number of limits, and at times more accurate analysis of a given phenomenon is achieved using other summary measures.

For instance, it may be desired to assess the return on a hectare of agricultural land over a given time period, say ten years. Returns on agricultural land may be influenced by numerous factors, such as weather. Over the ten-year period, it is reasonable to suppose that certain years will be characterized by particularly favorable weather conditions and others penalized by particularly adverse ones. In this case, it might be reasonable to exclude from yearly data outlying values, i.e. the lowest and the highest values, and to calculate the arithmetic mean for the remaining N-2 observations:

$$M_t = \frac{\sum_{i=2}^{9} x_i}{N-2}$$

The mean calculated in this way is known as the truncated mean.

Other examples of means provided by descriptive statistics are the geometric mean and the harmonic mean. The geometric mean is calculated by extracting the arithmetic root of index N of the results of all values:

$$M_g = \sqrt[N]{\prod_{i=1}^{N} x_i}$$

The geometric mean is a useful tool in strategic analysis for calculating, for instance, the average compound interest rate on a given investment. Let's suppose, for example, that in the last four years an investor has obtained from a given investment an interest rate equal to, respectively, 8% the first year, 10% the second year, 12% the third year and 9% the fourth year and that the investor would like to know which is the interest rate averagely obtained each year.

Because the values are percentage values, it is necessary to divide them for 100 and successively add to each value 1 in order to obtain the following multiplicative factors: 1.08, 1.10, 1.12, 1.09.

At this point we can calculate the geometric mean in the following way:

$$[1.08 \times 1.10 \times 1.12 \times 1.09]^{1/4} = 1.0974$$

By subtracting the value 1 to the result, and multiplying it by 100, the average compound interest rate, equal to 9.74%, is determined.

Less commonly used, on the other hand, is the harmonic mean; the latter is obtained from the reciprocal of the arithmetic mean of the reciprocals of the N values:

$$M_{ar} = \frac{N}{\sum_{i=1}^{N} \frac{1}{x_i}}$$

Another measure of considerable interest in strategic analysis is the median. The median is the value that separates observations on a given phenomenon into two sets with an equal number of observations (after arranging them in non-decreasing order).

The median is thus an indicator of position, one that represents central value in the distribution arranged in non-decreasing order; in other words, given N observations, the median is in position $\frac{N+1}{2}$ if N is odd and in positions $\frac{N}{2}$ and $\frac{N+1}{2}$ if N is even.

Therefore, for odd N the median is:

$$Me = x_{(\frac{N+1}{2})}$$

For even N, it is conventionally assumed that the central position is obtained by adding the two central values and dividing these by two; hence, the median is:

$$Me = \frac{x_{(\frac{N}{2})} + x_{(\frac{N+1}{2})}}{2}$$

The median also provides some very relevant information for the purposes of strategic analysis, information that is not supplied by any other mean. Take, for example, the distribution of revenues among a group of competing firms; some firms may have very high revenues, while many have rather low revenues. The median enables the analyst to determine which percentage of firms earns revenues above the median value. For example, it would be possible to say that 85% of firms has revenues equal to or below the median, and 15% revenues above the median.

Note that, in this case, the arithmetic mean may not be preferable to the median to indicate average revenues of firms in the sample, because the mean (given a few very high revenues and many low revenues) would show the revenue due to each firm if total revenues were divided into N equal parts, overestimating the revenues earned by more than half of the firms in the study.

Of the observations relating to a given phenomenon, the mode is the observation with the highest frequency: the more dominant the frequency of the mode, the more significant the information it provides. In the example in Table 2.2 the mode is Product 1 with a percentage frequency of 85%.

In the process of strategic analysis, the mode may be a useful tool with which to determine whether a most frequent observation exists for a given phenomena, and if so, which it is.

For example, if there is a desire to identify the geographical areas dominated by the direct competitors of a firm, the mode is the most useful tool because, in the light of revenues from different areas, the mode can identify, for each competitor, the most important geographical area.

Table 2.2   The Mode

Type of product sold	Frequency	Percentage frequency
Product 1	85,000	85%
Product 2	10,000	10%
Product 3	5,000	5%
Total products sold	100,000	100%

In this case also, the arithmetic mean would not shed any light on the distribution of revenues: Though it would indicate the average sales of direct competitors in the various geographical areas, it would not identify which was best guarded by competitors.

TOOLS BASED ON THE STUDY OF VARIABILITY AND MUTABILITY

The means outlined briefly involve a process of synthesis designed to substitute a set of observations on a given phenomenon with a single measure considered representative of the set. Means, in their various forms, are very useful tools in strategic analysis. However, they are unable to highlight one key aspect: the variability of data, or their mutability.

From a strategic perspective, it is very important to determine whether and to what extent a given observation differs from a reference value, typically a mean.

To satisfy this information need, descriptive statistics offers various methods that constitute useful and effective tools in a strategic context.

The most commonly used methods are the mean square error and the variance.

The mean square error represents the error of the intensities x_i from the arithmetic mean:

$$MS_a = \sigma = \left[\sqrt{\frac{\sum_1^N (x_i - M_a)^2}{N}} \right]$$

While the variance is none other than the mean square error squared:

$$\sigma^2 = \frac{\sum_1^N (x_i - M_a)^2}{N}$$

Because the most important contribution of this kind of instruments is to give some information about the distribution of data regarding a phenomenon, the analyst can usefully adopt the mean square error or the variance, when, for instance, he would like to know whether the sales of a product in different geographical areas, or in different period of times, are homogeneously distributed or present some values that significantly differ with the average value.

TOOLS BASED ON THE ANALYSIS OF RELATIONS BETWEEN TWO OR MORE VARIABLES

A problem of particular importance in strategic analysis is the understanding of the relation existing between two or more phenomena.

The branch of descriptive statistics that is concerned with the study of relations between two or more features is the multivariate descriptive statistics.

Among the numerous methods used in this branch of statistics, two are of special relevance as tools of strategic analysis, and it is these two tools that this section discusses: techniques based on the study of correlation and regression.

Techniques designed to analyze correlations between two variables seek to understand whether a linear association exists between the two. The existence and strength of the relation is expressed by the correlation coefficient.

The correlation coefficient is a number between -1 and 1 (-1 indicates asymmetric correlation: as one variable increases the other decreases; 1 indicates maximum correlation: the two variables move in the same direction; 0 denotes that the apparent relation between the two variables may be random). Given a set of observations between two variables x and y, the correlation coefficient may be calculated as follows:

$$r = \frac{\sum_{i=1}^{n}(x_i - \bar{x})(y_i - \bar{y})}{\sqrt{\sum_{i=1}^{n}(x_i - \bar{x})^2 \sum_{i=1}^{n}(y_i - \bar{y})}}$$

where:

$$\bar{x} = \frac{1}{n}\sum_{i=1}^{n}x_i \ ; \ \bar{y} = \frac{1}{n}\sum_{i=1}^{n}y_i$$

are sample means.

Consider, for example, the importance of determining the existence of a linear relation between investments in R&D and royalties due on a patent license agreement or the existence of a linear relation between investments in advertising and changes in sales.

Note that correlation analysis is unable to highlight the existence of a relation of causality, and merely determines whether a linear correlation exists. Two variables, for example, could be correlated symmetrically (as one varies, the other increases also) even though they are not linked by cause-effect relationship: it may be that both depend causally on a third variable that is, for both, an independent variable.

On the other hand, to understand the dependence of a (dependent) variable on another (independent) variable, regression analysis is used; it can be bivariate or multivariate according to the number (two or more than two) of variables that make it possible to explain the relation of causality.

It is beyond the scope of this chapter to discuss the technical formalization of regression analysis, for which the reader should refer to the specialist literature.

One particularly important use of linear regression relates to problems concerning the determination of the cost of capital and, in particular, the calculation of the β coefficient that expresses systematic risk for a given firm.

In the Capital Asset Pricing Model (CAPM), in fact, the β coefficient is estimated by relating the share price return to the market rate, by means of simple regression using the following formula:

$$R_j = \alpha + \beta \times R_m$$

where:

R_j is the share price return;
R_m is the market return;
α is the intercept of the regression. This parameter provides a measure of actual performance during the time period compared to the CAPM estimate;
β is the slope of the regression curve and measures the riskiness of a share.

In general, the β coefficient expresses how fluctuations in the economy translate into fluctuations in the share price return, increasing ($\beta > 1$), remaining unchanged ($\beta = 1$), or decreasing ($\beta < 1$) with respect to the overall market trend.

Finally, the existence of a cause-effect relation between two variables is often represented graphically on a Cartesian plane, to enhance the immediacy and efficacy of the result. For example, the reader may note herein industry life cycle analysis (Figure 2.1).

TOOLS BASED ON DEDUCTIVE LOGIC

In the strategic environment, deductive logic enables the analyst to highlight the relations among variables, and the effects of their interaction resulting from competitive phenomena.

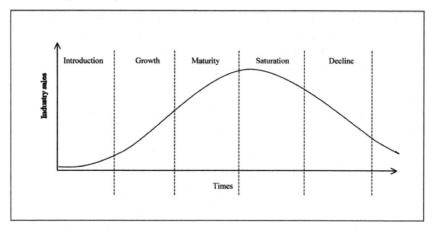

Figure 2.1   Industry life cycle.

The ultimate purpose of deductive analysis is to define a logically correct solution that is consistent with the deductive process. Some extensions of mathematical logic are functional to strategic analysis, and among these, game theory is of particular importance.

The application of game theory to strategic studies was the result of the extension of models of structural analysis to forms of competition (see Box 1, 'Strategic archetypes', in Chapter One). This fostered the adoption in strategic analysis of a number of innovative tools to assess the rational choices made by firms, in terms of the pay-offs (Ghemawat 1997).

Game theory is a mathematical approach to the study of interactions between two or more subjects that takes into account elements of conflict, cooperation and competition.

The aim of game theory is to identify the equilibria that can be reached in different relational situations, their causes and the actions taken as a consequence.

The assessment of risks and opportunities inherent in a competitive environment induces management to consider the actions and possible counter-actions of rivals. Through strategic reasoning, which is the ultimate objective of competition governing, management hypothesizes a set of reasonable and acceptable pay-offs to be had by implementing strategies that take into account the dynamics of the competitive environment. Game theory is a useful tool that combines the ability to look forward and reason backward to interpret economic incentives.

The key aspects that guide strategic reasoning through the application of game theory can be summarized in three stages:

1. definition of the strategic action that a firm wishes to pursue, for example, penetration of a new market or the acquisition of a new business unit, and investigate further if the strategic action is correlated

at the same time to other market-related decisions, by modifying the structure of demand, the cost function or barriers to entry;

2. assessment of relative competitors to determine whether and to what extent these are influenced by the strategic action. At this stage, it is important to consider carefully network effects on suppliers and distributors. Furthermore, it is necessary to assess the objectives and strategic options available to competitors;

3. definition of the competitive game, be it a simultaneous or a sequential game, and the relative weight of the choices of the leader and the follower.

Note, however, that recourse to game theory as a tool of strategic analysis may bring benefits not only by defining potential strategic options and by managing information flows optimally, but also serve, as a useful logical exercise in predicting further developments in competitive dynamics.

Because the dimensions of the decision-making process are highly complex, game theory has elaborated various game models:

1. static or dynamic games, depending on whether individuals move simultaneously or sequentially;

2. games with complete or incomplete information, depending on whether all players are aware of the function that determines pay-offs for each set of choices made by other players, or incomplete if at least one player is uncertain of results that can be achieved by another (in Bayesian games, calculations of probability are made in attempt to resolve problems);

3. games that can be represented graphically by means of matrices or trees; generally, matrices are used for static games, while extensive forms or trees are used for dynamic games, though this distinction is not fixed and both forms may be used in the different types of interaction.

The increasingly dynamic and variable economic environment, and the numerous factors of environmental turbulence, have led to an increase in the demand for analytical skills and tools to deploy in strategic analysis. One solution is to exploit game theory to analyze a series of consequences in terms of the pay-offs that can be achieved from a range of choices made by sufficiently informed rational agents. Thanks to the deductive framework upon which game theory rests, it is possible to summarize the advantages and disadvantages of each choice, and to make comparisons with the options available to competitors in the various scenarios that may follow on from a strategic action. Game theory is not only a mathematical tool that generates a specific response; it is also a technique that can support managerial decisions in a strategic and analytical process.

3 Qualitative Tools of Strategic Analysis

Giulia Solinas and Silvia Vernizzi

The qualitative (or 'soft') tools used in strategic analysis differ from their quantitative counterparts in terms of the underlying methodology that does not produce a numerical summary measure. In fact, the output of qualitative analysis can be represented flexibly by means of a multitude of logical schemes and explanatory diagrams of a descriptive nature. Qualitative methodology has important uses in strategic analysis, enabling the analyst to understand the essential characteristics of the phenomenon under investigation and to organize the mass of data, whilst remaining readily adaptable to the specific needs of the project.

This chapter is structured in the following parts:

- methodology and description for the classification of tools
- causation and feedback qualitative tools
- causation and contextualization qualitative tools
- causation and correlation qualitative tools

METHODOLOGY AND DESCRIPTION FOR THE CLASSIFICATION OF TOOLS

The decision to adopt a qualitative rather than a quantitative tool depends on the nature of the strategic issue. Indeed, it may be necessary to provide a detailed description of variables, a result that quantitative methodology, inherently oriented towards summary measures, does not foresee. Numerical indexes or regression coefficients are the outcome of a methodology that seeks to capture in a single measure a complete relation or the expected trend of a strategic phenomenon. Conversely, certain phenomena cannot be conveyed by a summary measure, being typically related to contingencies, and call for qualitative analysis that set outs relations and logical flows in descriptive terms. Qualitative methodology allows the description of basic variables, the logical categories to which they belong, and the properties underlying the logical relations. Finally, a fundamental aspect of qualitative methodology is its communicative impact that differs significantly from quantitative methodology.

The qualitative approach is based on an inductive process of reasoning that initially seeks to make sense of phenomena. The qualitative approach views the problem or processes being analyzed as constantly shifting contingencies that the analyst needs to reconstruct and interpret in a logical and comprehensive manner. In the exploration of strategic phenomena, the quantitative approach emphasizes words rather than numerical expressions, the principal aim being qualification of strategic phenomena rather than the quantification typically provided by quantitative tools.

Qualitative methodology proceeds through:

- an initial mental definition of the problem, resulting in the identification of common factors;
- further investigation of the explanatory features in an iterative process until the logical validity of the model is confirmed;

The strategic tools used in a qualitative approach are functional to:

- data reduction: coding, segmenting and summarizing the dataset;
- data display: organizing, compressing and assembling the dataset to abstract and compare multi-level concepts;
- data interpretation: relevant concepts are developed and used to make sense of general phenomena. This stage depends on the analyst's expertise and the complexity of the contingencies affecting the strategic phenomena. The main risks inherent in data interpretation are subjectivity of analysis and lack of transparency. In the first case, findings rely too heavily on the analyst's view of what is significant and important, and his stance in relation to the contingencies. A lack of transparency makes it difficult to assess how the analyst arrived at the conclusions, and may be the result of ambiguity in the use of strategic tools, or of an unclear view of the logic underlying the analyst's reasoning (Bryman and Bell 2007).

Finally, qualitative tools make it possible both to describe the competitive phenomenon being analyzed, and to make inferences on the strategic variables.

Qualitative tools may be of two types that can be mapped on the basis of:

1. dynamic logic: this type of tool makes it possible to process data and obtain an overview of the dynamics between the variables identified by the analyst. Such tools can be labelled 'causation and feedback tools', and are fundamental for capturing in descriptive form the retroactive phenomena arising from a strategic decision, positive or negative synergies and interconnections between information flows in an organization. Flow charts and impact wheels are examples of causation and feedback tools;
2. static logic: this type of tool provides an accurate snapshot of the precise moment in which variables and key concepts are analyzed. Such tools can be subdivided into:
   - tools designed to represent diagrammatically key concepts and variables on the basis of cardinal dimensions identified by the

analyst, without actually summarizing the concepts and variables in an index number, or relating them to each other. These can be defined 'causation and contextualization tools'; two examples are PEST analysis and the SWOT matrix;

- tools that seek to describe the bi-dimensional relation between two variables in a given time horizon. These can be defined 'causation and correlation tools'; two notable examples are the Boston Consulting Group matrix and the strategy clock.

CAUSATION AND FEEDBACK
QUALITATIVE TOOLS: DIAGRAMS

These tools seek to analyze the logical connections embedded in strategic information, to map the complexity of the strategic phenomena being investigated and to sketch the fundamental relations affecting the variables. Organizations need to disentangle the causal ambiguity inherent in adapting to changing situations, a factor that shapes the competitive environment (Schwaninger 2009). However, it is first necessary to map the systemic problems giving rise to internal and external organizational complexity, to underscore the key dimensions of strategic analysis, and to provide a correlated analysis of the variables. Diagrams are conceptual tools that support the analytical process of disentangling the complexity and variety of strategic phenomena; furthermore, they provide a multi-dimensional framework that enables the analyst to further his understanding of causality and feedback.

Diagrams are an application of logic used extensively in cybernetics and business management, being well-suited to immediate and unambiguous description of the logical relations affecting strategic phenomena. Diagrams are unique in that they enable the analyst to re-elaborate information contained in what initially appears a shapeless mass into flows and to identify the paths linking the cardinal variables in the dataset. Diagrams can be used in several stages of strategic analysis:

- in the preliminary stages of analysis to identify variables and causal relations;
- to assess changes in relations between variables. In this case, the analyst aims to study the effects and impact of dynamic variations in one or more variables on the whole system.

Several types of diagrams are used in strategic analysis:

- impact wheel diagrams
- flow diagrams
- system charts

Impact Wheel Diagrams

Impact wheel diagrams trace the multi-level effects of an event or trend. They are structured, in the sense that they build several linear paths of effects originating from a strategic phenomenon. Clearly, a primary effect can extend beyond boundaries and overlap with other effects. Impact wheels help the analyst to assess the complexity of such effects and their trends. Figure 3.1 presents a general example of an impact wheel diagram.

As Figure 3.1 shows, impact wheel diagrams enable the analyst to sketch the causal relations between strategic events at the same time as causes and effects. This strategic tool also makes it possible to introduce a temporal dimension, bringing together in a multi-level perspective several phenomena that may not appear straightforwardly connected. In this sense, strategic phenomena may be analyzed from different perspectives, denoted by gray circles in Figure 3.1, which do not unambiguously define a set of outcomes, but that can themselves be investigated in greater detail. Figure 3.1 presents only two levels of concentric circles reflecting the degree of analytical complexity of the example, but this type of framework can be adapted to a range of situations by adding concentric circles or increasing the number of analytical factors contemplated at each level and creating links between them.

Flow Diagrams

The main purpose of flow diagrams is to express an algorithm; they focus on transforming initial data to deliver an output. What is unique about this type of diagram is their ability to effectively process a series of variables to arrive at an unambiguous result. Flow diagrams are widely used in information technology, while their application in strategic contexts is more restricted. They may be employed, for example, to evaluate resource utilization in productive processes; in this case, flow diagrams facilitate analysis of the logical sequence of processes within the organization, making it possible to rule out overlapping and inefficiencies.

Flow charts exhibit certain weaknesses that may trouble the strategic analyst, despite being powerful tools for analyzing the logical sequence of strategic processes and activities. A major weakness is their focus on logical sequences independently of timing, a highly relevant feature in strategic analysis. So flow diagrams need to be complemented by other tools that safeguard the temporal dimension. In a nutshell, flow charts trace the underlying causes of a problem and may help to make sense of them.

System Charts

System charts present relations between variables in terms of causality and reacting impacts, in the form of a closed chain of causes and effects. These

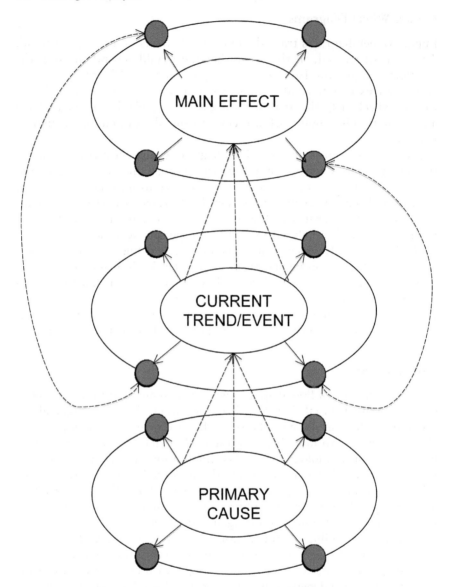

Figure 3.1   Impact wheel diagram. Source: Adaptation from Coyle G., 2006.

tools enable the analyst to highlight the positive or negative nature of relations and the cumulative effect that a set of variables may induce on a
certain phenomenon in terms of sign polarity. System charts are based on
loops; these exist if it is possible to connect one variable to others and
return to the starting point without passing any point more than once.
Loops can have positive or negative signs: a positive sign denotes a positive
causal relationship, whereas a negative sign reflects a negative goal-seeking

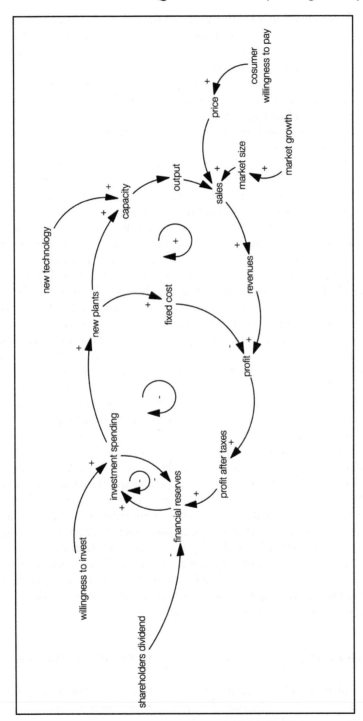

Figure 3.2   System Charts.

connection. The polarity of the circular relation is the result of multiplying signs with basic algebraic rules. Timing is taken into account by inserting delays in connections. System charts underscore the significance of feedback analysis and are the basis of quantitative simulation analysis, being tools that serve in both qualitative and quantitative analysis. System charts also reduce complexity by tracing variables and their effects on a single sheet of paper, so all relevant factors and causal relations are simultaneously visible in a reasoned presentation of the various dynamics impacting the strategic phenomenon.

System charts are widely used in strategic analysis (Coyle 2004), in view of their extreme flexibility and the immediate reading they provide of, for example, the rise of a new technology, or the impact on an organization of changes in the supply chain. A short and intuitive example of how system charts can be used is presented in this chapter in figure 3.2. It concerns the investment strategy of a generic firm wishing to undertake a new investment to boost internal growth. The new investment enhances output capacity and enables the firm to satisfy product demand. Sales increase, with a positive impact on profits, and, ultimately, on financial reserves, hence polarity is positive. On the other hand, the new investment results in an increase in fixed costs, with a negative impact on profits and a negative sign among variables. The net outcome of the investment strategy depends on the sum of the polarities; it may be influenced by external factors such as the distribution of dividends to shareholders, or consumers' willingness to pay. A dynamic diagram, in this case, makes the analyst aware of overall connections and any ambiguity in terms of final results. The model can be made more sophisticated by adding further variables; here, the aim was to offer insight into this type of tool.

It is worth mentioning that several other diagrams can be used to analyze the complexity and causality of strategic phenomena. As Coyle (2004) asserts, many techniques and tools exist because they serve in specific contexts and the core statements of diagrams may be adapted to specific contingencies. The aim of the present survey of the various diagrams was to offer a preliminary insight on the form of available tools. Those wishing to explore diagrams more thoroughly will find a vast literature, including numerous applicative examples (see, for instance, Warren 2008). Finally, the relevance of diagrams lies in their ability to make sense of complex processes and strategic activities. Sometimes an impact wheel will provide sufficient insight to the analyst; if it does not, then it can be combined with system charts that enable the analyst to identify the dynamics underlying the strategic phenomenon.

CAUSATION AND CONTEXTUALIZATION QUALITATIVE TOOLS

This type of tool seeks to identify variables relevant to the description of a phenomenon without the use of a quantitative summary measure, and without relating variables to one another.

Such tools enable the analyst to describe and schematize phenomena by identifying the multiple factors that, from various perspectives, provide a sufficiently complete picture of the problem.

The advantage of causation and contextualization tools is the immediacy of the description they provide that can be further elaborated using other quantitative and qualitative tools.

One of the best-known examples is, undoubtedly, Porter's five forces framework identifying the five forces that determine the attractiveness of an industry: customers, suppliers, competitors, potential entrants and producers of substitutive products (Porter 1980). It allows a very simple and immediate description, providing the firm with a snapshot of the relevant industry. Further detail can be added, in relation to specific needs, by using other tools. For example, each force may be summarized by one or more quantitative variables that enable the analyst to assign a value to the impact of each force on the overall attractiveness of the industry.

Two further examples of this type of tool are PEST analysis (and its extension PESTEL) and SWOT analysis. PEST or PESTEL analysis is a strategic tool that seeks to identify structural drivers of change; in other words, factors that in various way can or could affect the structure of an industry in future and, consequently, the strategic choices of firms and related outcomes (Narayanan and Fahey 2001).

Specifically, PESTEL analysis (Figure 3.3) classifies critical variables into four main types: political, economic, social and technological, whereas PESTEL analysis adds two further categories of variables: environmental and legal.

Each of the four (or six) types of variables are not static but may change over time and in relation to the competitive context. A factor that is relevant at one time in a given competitive space may not be relevant in a different spatial or temporal context.

Moreover, although critical variables are identified separately and subsequently classified into types, to interpret the competitive context correctly they should be considered jointly: very often it is the combined effect of separate factors that is important, rather than the individual effects of variables.

SWOT analysis is a strategic tool that summarizes the 'key strategic messages' arriving from the business environment and from within the firm; in other words, the firm's strategic competences in the sense of its unique and unrepeatable combination of resources and capabilities.

These key strategic messages are summarized into four categories: strengths, weaknesses (relating to the internal characteristics of the firm), opportunities and threats (relating to the business environment).

The aim is to identify the extent to which current strengths and weaknesses are relevant to, and capable of managing, changes taking place in the business environment. SWOT analysis can also be used to assess the opportunities a firm should exploit or the threats from which it should defend itself.

POLITYCAL ANALYSIS	ECONOMIC ANALYSIS	SOCIAL ANALYSIS	TECHNOLOGICAL ANALYSIS	ENVIRONMENTAL ANALYSIS	LEGAL ANALYSIS
Political stability	Type of economic system in countries of operation	Demographics	Recent technological developments	Environmental protection laws	Monopolies legislation
Risk of military invasion	Government intervention in the free market	Class structure	Technology's impact on product offering	Waste disposal	Employment law
	Efficiency of financial markets	Education	Impact on cost structure	Energy consumption	Health and safety
	Infrastructure quality	Culture (gender roles, etc)	Impact on value chain structure		Product safety
	Skill level of workforce	Entrepreneurial spirit	Rate of technological diffusion		Intellectual property protection
	Labor cost	Attitudes			Trade regulations and tariffs
	Business cycle stage	Leisure interests			Anti trust laws
	Economic growth rate				Taxation – tax rates and incentives
	Inflation rate				Wage legislation

Figure 3.3 PESTEL analysis.

Overall, SWOT analysis should help focus discussion on future choices and the extent to which the single firm is capable of sustaining its strategies (Ansoff 1968; Ambrosini, Johnson, and Scholes 1998; Johnson and Scholes 2002).

Two examples of SWOT analysis are presented in Figure 3.4, relating to two major firms operating at a global level: Luxottica in the eyewear sector and Swatch in the watch industry.

CAUSATION AND CORRELATION QUALITATIVE TOOLS

These tools, unlike those presented earlier, do not seek exclusively to identify variables relevant to the description of a phenomenon; rather, they outline the relation between variables at a given moment in time. In other words, they attempt to highlight, from a qualitative perspective, the effects deriving from a combination of two or more variables. Examples of such tools are the 'BCG matrix' and the 'strategy clock'.

The BCG matrix aims to describe the characteristics of a firm's portfolio of activities (The Boston Consulting Group Inc., 1973). The BCG matrix is grounded on the assumption that to guarantee the creation of economic value in the long term, a firm's business portfolio should contain elements with diverse growth prospects, investment needs and capacity to generate liquidity. Only the diversity and complementariness of the various activities can assure the equilibrium essential to long-term survival.

Departing from this assumption, two dimensions are identified: the firm's market share and the growth rate of the specific business area.

The intersection of these two dimensions makes it possible to identify four types of activity as shown in Figure 3.5.

1. stars: activities with a high growth rate, in which the firm has a high market share. This type of business has the potential for good profit margins in the long term but requires substantial investments to finance development;
2. question marks: activities for which the firm has a low market share but which have a high growth rate. They are known as question marks because they are the most uncertain types of business: Sustained by high levels of investment to increase market share, they could become stars, but without adequate investment they may be incapable of generating positive income and cash flows, turning into dogs;
3. dogs: low growth, low market share activities. They do not generate, in the long term at least, positive income flows; consequently, management should divest to dedicate resources to activities with better growth prospects;
4. cash cows: low growth activities in which the firm has a large market share. They require lower levels of investment and generate a great deal of liquidity that can be used to finance other areas of business.

LUXOTTICA GROUP S.P.A

STRENGHTS	WEAKNESSES
Enhancing customer recall and market share with a portfolio of strong brand names. Driving growth through innovation and focus on R&D. Strong distribution network and further investment in enhancing market presence gives Luxottica a competitive edge over its peer group.	Weak financial performance adversely affects the shareholders confidence and also impedes Luxottica's further expansion plans. Geographic concentration for revenue generation and dependence on a small supplier base.

OPPORTUNITIES	THREATS
Increasing efficiency in business operations through the implementation of Systems Applications and Products in Data Processing (SAP). Growing market presence with licensing agreements as well as acquisitions. Increasing demand for optical products as the percentage of ageing population grows in various countries.	Rampant existence of counterfeit products dilutes the group's brand image and deprives it of revenue growth. Growing preference for laser eye surgery could adversely impact the group's revenues.

THE SWATCH GROUP LTD.

STRENGHTS	WEAKNESSES
Global market presence. Strong brand equity. Diversified product portfolio.	Declining operating efficiency.

OPPORTUNITIES	THREATS
Strategic initiative. Emerging Indian market. Growth through opening new stores.	Strong competition. Exchange rate risk.

Figure 3.4   Examples of SWOT analysis.

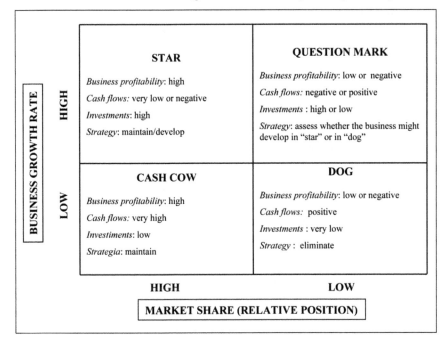

Figure 3.5   The Boston Consulting Group matrix.

These tools therefore provide the firm with an immediate description of the activities it pursues and the characteristics of each in terms of investments, income, funding needs and ability to generate liquidity. Observation of such activities and their relative composition offers directions for future portfolio choices.

The 'strategy clock' intends to indicate how a firm can gain a competitive advantage over its competitors (Faulkner and Bowman 1995).

As Chapter Four explains, a firm has a competitive advantage over its rivals when it supplies a product or service perceived as the best by potential buyers (a differentiation advantage) or when it supplies a product or service at a lower cost than its rivals (a cost advantage).

The strategy clock departs from this definition of competitive advantage to identify two possible ways to gain a competitive advantage:

- act on the price perceived by potential buyers;
- act on the selling price, on the implicit assumption that a lower selling price reflects a firm's efficiency and that a high selling price is indicative of a firm with high costs.

By combining these two dimensions, the strategy clock identifies eight potential strategic choices (Figure 3.6).

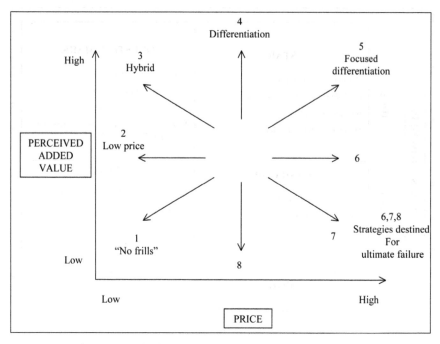

Figure 3.6   The strategy clock.

1. no frills strategy: This combines low costs with low perceived value. Though apparently unattractive, it may in fact be a winning strategy in price-sensitive market segments where consumers recognize the not excellent quality of a product or service yet consciously choose the product or service because, for that type of consumer, the benefits to be had from a low price compensate the disadvantage of low quality. One example of the application of this type of strategy is no-frills airlines;

2. low price strategy: this aims to supply a product with a low price (implicitly indicating efficiency) and a perceived value similar to that of rival products;

3. hybrid strategy: one of the most difficult strategies to pursue, because it aims to maintain costs below those of rivals, keeping prices low, and at the same time to differentiate the firm from rivals in terms of perceived value. A winning example of this type of strategy is IKEA in the home furnishings sector.;

4. differentiation strategy: this aims to supply products and services perceived to be better than rival products and services at a price similar to that of competitors;

5. focus differentiation strategy: this seeks to offer a product with a high perceived value and a high price, usually in a specific market segment. Take, for example, Apple computers in the personal computer market:

The high-quality technical, functional and aesthetic characteristics of the products are associated with, and justify, a high price;

6., 7., 8. the last three strategies in the strategic clock are, unlike those previously mentioned, losing strategies, destined to fail in the attempt to gain a competitive advantage. These strategies combine a high price with a low perceived value of the product or service.

CONCLUSIONS

It has been seen that there are numerous tools of strategic analysis that rely on quantitative methodology; these can essentially be classified in two macro categories: those based on dynamic logic and those based on static logic.

Both types of tools aim to describe, present or schematize a phenomenon, offering management the most complete picture possible of factors relevant to strategic decisions.

Qualitative tools are entirely different to those based on quantitative methodology that provide a numerical summary measure. Nevertheless, despite their differences, the two types of tools should not be considered alternatives, but rather complementary to each another. Indeed, a combination of the two types, in relation to the specific knowledge needs and the availability of information, provides management with the informational framework needed to make strategic management decisions.

4 The Competitive Structure

This chapter is devoted to understanding more thoroughly the competitive structure, namely the individual elements that compose it, which are:

- the combination of resources, capabilities and strategic competences
- the production technology portfolio
- the competitive position
- the configuration of the competitive processes
- the competitive arenas
- the critical success factors, the factors of strength and relative weakness
- the resulting competitive positions.

THE COMBINATION OF RESOURCES, CAPABILITIES AND STRATEGIC COMPETENCES

With the *Resource Based View* (RBV) studies, we understand the importance that resources have in determining choices and competitive results. Leaving aside the many precursors, the RBV research field acquires contours as defined in the Wernefelt article of 1984, which developed the concept of competitive barriers due to the asymmetric availability of resources (Wernefelt 1984). According to Wernefelt, these barriers are generated when the experience in using resources reduces the costs for active competitors and raises them for potential newcomers. A theoretical framework progressively takes form in which the competitive position of the company is directly related to the possession of resources (Barney 1986), which are:

- not homogeneously distributed among competitors
- not perfectly mobile (Peteraf 1993).

The combined effect of heterogeneity and imperfect mobility of resources is the basis of competitive differentiation between economic players and the consequent differences in income results obtained. Of course, the resources, which being heterogeneous and not perfectly mobile could trigger a mechanism of competitive differentiation, have specific characteristics. The so-called VRIO framework identifies these characteristics as the value, rarity, non-imitable status and organizational orientation (Barney 1991, Barney and Griffin 1992).

For the purposes of strategic analysis, a resource is of value (valuable) when it allows the company to reduce its costs or seize opportunities, or even neutralize the threats posed by competitive environments in which it operates (Barney 1991, Newbert 2008).

Resources can only relatively take on these features—that is, only in relation to a specific space-time combination, namely in relation to a particular competitive context (Cockburn and Henderson 2000). To build advantageous positions, a resource should also be rare—that is, owned by a limited number of competitors, current and potential. According to Barney this number must be low enough to prevent competitive forms close to perfect competition (Barney 1991). This requirement naturally has to do with competitive heterogeneity: If a valuable resource were widely distributed among competitors, it would then become necessary to compete but it could not be the source of distinguishing competitive positions between incumbents. The rarity, however, is not entirely sufficient to explain favorable long-term competitive positions. In fact, a rare and valuable resource could still be copied and reproduced. The key question then is: 'How easily and quickly can a rare and valuable resource be copied and reproduced?'

The more mechanisms of isolation that interact, the more difficult and expensive the process of imitation becomes and the more the rare and valuable resource continues to be protected and to generate beneficial effects for those who possess it. In RBV studies, many phenomena generate mechanisms of isolation, including in particular the following:

- the presence of strong 'causal ambiguity', which prevents competitors from understanding what the relationship is between resources and competitive behavior;
- the level of idiosyncrasy of resources, which, if high, makes the wealth of information and knowledge poorly mobile or transferable;
- the presence of formal arrangements for the legal protection of resource use (for example, a trademark or patent);
- the time necessary for competitors to activate mechanisms of imitation, meaning that the longer this period of time, the more opportunities left to the *first mover* to strengthen its competitive position and protect its resource assets;
- other phenomena such as economies of scale, learning curves, the size of firms—in short, anything that can significantly generate information asymmetry (Dierickx and Cool 1989, Sun and Tse 2009).

Finally, the last item considered by the VRIO framework is represented by organizational orientation, which specifically means business capabilities, namely that applied body of knowledge that allows the business to conduct the transformation processes necessary for the preparation of a competitive supply system (Amit and Schoemaker 1993). Whereas resources are a stock of assets (including intangible ones), capabilities are the means (patterns of action) with which firms systematically and stably use (render active) resources. In other words, capabilities, or skills, are also resources that make every other resource productive and purposeful in the company's economy; they are a flow of knowledge that moves the stock of resources (Zott 2003). Thus, while valuable, rare and hard to imitate resources intrinsically have the potential to generate competitive advantages, capabilities have the ability to transform potentials into benefits (Newbert 2008). One can arrive at the conclusion that a business is represented by a set of resources 'in action' by examining a last and important component—strategic competences (Hamel and Prahalad 1990, Hamel and Prahalad 1993, Sanchez 2001).

Competencies include organizational capabilities that allow a coordinated use of all resources, including capabilities, and which is above all directly responsible for competitive advantage positions. Whereas capabilities may play a very general role in a business' activities on all levels, strategic competences are those capabilities that make the difference on the competitive level. We can assume that strategic competences are the synthesis of the VRIO framework and that they derive from an encounter between resources that have certain characteristics (value, rarity, inimitability) and the capabilities able to mobilize them (Hitt et al. 2005) (Figure 4.1).

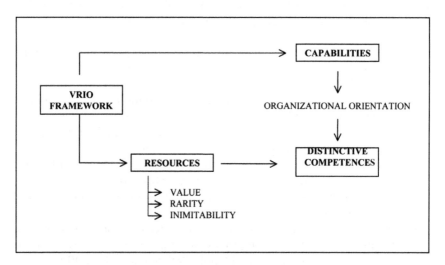

Figure 4.1   Resources, capabilities and strategic competences.

Strategic competences seem to have three basic characteristics:

- they are typically customer-oriented to ensure buyers are provided with high value output. In other words, those who possess these competences seem to understand customer needs and desires better and more quickly than others do;
- they are future-oriented, rather than directed to the needs of the present, in that they endow those who have these competences with the superior capability to grasp contextual trends in advance or even influence them;
- they have extensibility compared to the competitive arenas in which the firm already operates. That is, they are not competences specifically employed to meet a need and thus functional to a sole position, but abilities that can be decisive for any positioning, present or future.

As the first element in the competitive structure, the combination of resources, capabilities and strategic competences is also the most profound and often the most difficult part to assess in a company's strategic identity. They take shape over time and are the result of competitive choices and results obtained. At the same time they affect both current and future choices and the probability of achieving desired results.

THE PRODUCTION TECHNOLOGY PORTFOLIO

The production technology portfolio consists of knowledge applied to 'how to do what', thus knowledge of the processes needed to make products and services. Among the choices that characterize the competitive structure, those concerning the production portfolio are normally more rooted in the company's culture; any substantial change to the portfolio would mean that a company would have to face diversification processes.

For a long time it was thought that a given product, the result of specific technology, and a satisfied need were linked by a two-way relationship; that is, that every technological system of production (nature of the product/service) corresponded to one and only one system of demand, and vice versa. Consequently, the industry, which Marshall defined as a set of firms offering an identical product, also identifies the borders of competitive space. Today, however, technology and demand follow evolutionary paths that are not necessarily aligned. Let's try, for the sake of simplicity, to reconstruct the way an industry originates and evolves. The economic success of a productive technological paradigm initially coincides with a need or demand that gives origin to and corresponds to the original and general features of the technology market. In the automotive industry, for example, the technologies needed to build a car (productive technological paradigm) correspond to the original need for private transport; in the publishing industry, publishing technologies originated from the demand for content acquisition; in the pharmaceutical industry, applied bio-chemical technologies originated from the need for medical care, and so on. In other words, the industry forms because a greater or lesser number of companies use a homogeneous productive technological paradigm to meet a need.

The perfect match between product and need does not necessarily last for long after the start up of the industry, because significant changes may occur over time due to two phenomena:

1. the original needs branch off into derivative needs—partial or advanced needs—in relation to the original need;
2. different technological equipments (and thus different industries) converge on the same needs (original, but, more frequently, derivatives).

Although for different reasons, both phenomena have the same effect. Industry (technology) and competitive space (that is, all the firms in direct competition to meet the same need) do not always coincide (at least not perfectly); firms operating in the same field and in the same geographic area may not even be in competition with each other just as companies from different industries can come into competition on specific needs (technological convergence).

Although distinct from the competitive space, industries remain relevant and useful objects in strategic analyses because they are associated with a defined structure, namely a set of basic economic production characteristics, which usually concern all companies operating in the same industry.

INDUSTRY STRUCTURE

Industry structure is the basic set of features acquired from the supply of a particular type of product/service and its demand. In general terms, the importance of structural phenomena lies in the power they have in determining the competitive rules of the game; a different game is played in each industry. In Porter's expanded competition model, the industry's competitive structure is due to five macro aggregates (intensity of competition, level of bargaining power of suppliers and customers, potential newcomers, the availability of substitute products/services), which at any given time have a specific and variable configuration, dependent on so-called structural determinants. For each macro aggregate, Porter defines the main determinants as follows:

- intensity of competition: fragmentation and number of competitors present in the system, industry life cycle, the degree of diversity of products and services offered, level of fixed costs, mobility and output barriers;

- bargaining power of customers and suppliers: fragmentation of supply and demand markets; availability of substitute products, for customers or the company in relation to suppliers; level of customer and supplier integration; price sensitivity; brand identity (of the company for customers and of the supplier for the company); information available to the customer and the supplier; the importance of sold products/services for the customer, and importance of the purchased products/services for the company;
- potential newcomers: economy of scale and amount of capital required to start a business, the ease of access to required technological knowledge and specific production requirements (for instance, raw materials), experience and learning, access to distribution channels, brand strength, legislative actions to protect the competitive system against newcomers or, on the contrary, to promote them;
- availability of substitute products/services: abundance of substitute products/services, to a large extent dependent on the specificity of a combination of the needs and technology that characterizes the industry: price of alternative offers; the buyer's propensity to substitutes.

Acting on the five competitive forces (customers and suppliers are two distinct forces), the determinants shape the industry structure.

Industrial economic research has made it possible to understand more thoroughly an important aspect of structural dynamics concerning entry barrier functions, namely the costs that could affect newcomers but not the businesses already operating in the industry (incumbents). Industries are protected by entry barriers that create distortions in the mechanisms of market equilibrium and which have a direct impact on business profitability. An industry would have no entry barriers if potential newcomers could (Baumol et al. 1982):

- access the same technology and serve the same market under the same conditions as incumbent businesses;
- assess whether it is worth entering at the prices charged by incumbent businesses.

Examples of structural barriers, caused by the basic structure of an industry (productive technological paradigm) are the minimum production scale, the average cost of research and development, access to technological knowledge, control of critical resources and regulations. In addition to these barriers, industrial economists have classified other entrance costs that they consider strategic barriers, deliberately induced by competitors to discourage the entry of new businesses in a given industry (Besanko et al. 2002). To be exact, this deterrent behavior may follow two different lines:

- they are intended to strengthen and support the structural barriers;

- they create new barriers (in this sense they would be strategic barriers) through specific conducts concerning, for instance, the price or the maintenance of excess production capacity (Lieberman 1987).

In his pioneering work, Bain (Bain 1951) made a distinction between structural barriers and strategic barriers to identify three different entry situations (and related barriers):

- accommodated entry: when structural barriers are virtually nonexistent and the cost of creating strategic barriers is higher than the likely benefits;
- deterred entry: when structural barriers are low, the cost of creating strategic barriers is lower than the likely benefits; competitors give rise to what Fisher calls 'predatory acts' (Fischer 1991);
- blockaded entry: when the impact of the structural barriers is so significant that competitors will not try to raise additional strategic barriers.

If the structure significantly determines the importance of the entry barriers to an industry, the barriers, in turn, are the reasons for the average profitability of the industry.

Between 1990 and 1999, several publications tried, on empirical grounds, to clearly define what lies at the roots of the phenomena of profitability and extra profitability by analyzing the variance in profitability for a population of business units, which they used as the primary source for collecting economic and financial data. The first to do this type of research was Schmalensee, who analyzed the results obtained in 1975 from US manufacturing firms, as reported in the *Federal Trade Commission's Line of Business Report* database. Several scholars continued along these lines, each time refining the statistical modeling and the choice of the test sample. In these studies, the operating profits at the business unit level was broken down using different measurement techniques and logic, in order to trace it mainly:

- to industry profitability (industry effect);
- to membership in a multi-business system (corporate parent effects);
- to specific phenomena of the business unit under analysis (a firm's specific effects, or even business unit effect).

The research, conducted with specific statistical and analytical models and using different databases, did not always lead to consistent results. However, the variance in the results obtained from business units (or segments) was generally due (Wernefelt 1984, Schmalensee 1985, Montgomery 1988, Rumelt 1991, Roquebert et al. 1996, Power 1996, McGahan and Porter 1997):

- to a greater extent, to specific phenomena of the business unit itself (between 30% and 45% of the variance of the results obtained by individual business units);
- to a lesser yet still significant extent, to industry phenomena (between 10% and 20%);
- to a negligible extent, to the role of corporate (between 1% and 5%).

For example, in Anita McGahan and Michael Porter's analytical model (McGahan and Porter 1997) the profitability r of a given business segment (contrary to the business units such as those used by Rumelt (1991)) obtained in accordance with US GAAP, is thus represented:

$$r_{i,k,t} = \mu + \gamma_t + \alpha_i + \beta_k + \phi_{i,k} + \varepsilon_{i,k,t}$$

$r_{i,k,t}$: operating margin (operating income over assets) of the business segment created by business k in industry i in year t;

μ: average profitability achieved by all business segments analyzed in entire period of study;

γ_t: the difference between μ and the average profitability of all business segments analyzed in year t;

α_i: increased results associated with presence in industry i;

β_k: increased results associated with belonging to company k;

$\phi_{i,k}$: increased results associated with the specific situation of the business k, in industry i;

$\varepsilon_{i,k,t}$: residual profitability components.

The results obtained in this study suggest that operating profitability is:

- 18% due to the industry structure to which it belongs;
- 32% due to the competitive position in the industry;
- 4.33% due to the corporate effect;
- 2.39% due to the time effect;
- 42.89% due to other phenomena, exogenous to the model.

THE CHOSEN COMPETITIVE POSITIONING

Having one or more production technologies does not mean having chosen how to address the competition, if not minimally. Through the choice of competitive positioning, the company decides how to use its technological assets to meet specific needs. Positioning choices are the result of three integrated decisions concerning (Figure 4.2):

- the segmentation of supply in question, or even competitive segmentation (the 'what' of positioning);
- the geographic target areas of supply (the 'where' of positioning);
- the type of distinction pursued (the 'how' of positioning).

When building positioning in these three areas, two other variables come into play that needs to be consistent with each other and the positioning itself.

First, the product, as seen in a technological sense, has already been described. The choice of products concerns:

- their nature (the type of product/service);
- their amplitude (range);
- their extension, that is, the degree of vertical integration (how much space you occupy in the wider supply chain).

Second, one must identify the consumer (demand), which appears to be a logical consequence of the choice of product to supply, the geographic area and distinction. For example, a software designed by an Italian non-profit organization has been available since 2008 to make using a computer to

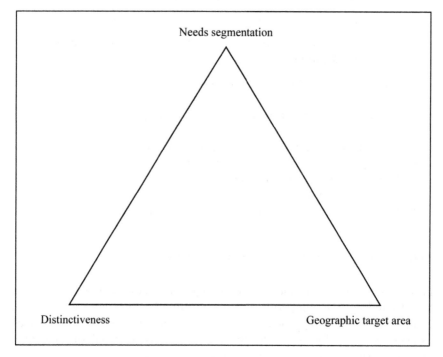

Figure 4.2   Choices of competitive positioning.

surf the Internet quite simple (an interface with six large keys). The software was specifically designed for people over sixty years old who have long begun to use the computer to access the Internet (in particular social networks and Skype). The program, which has been translated into twenty-two languages, creates a very efficient meeting point between positioning (with a new demand), technology and customer identity (although in this case the software is available free of charge). Let us now take a closer look at the three areas of competitive positioning.

THE SEGMENTATION OF NEEDS

Concerning the first area of positioning, the firm chooses, for each specific kind of technology available, its position relative to the original need, choosing in particular:

- whether to provide a product or service without any segmentation or specific segmentation (thus providing it, you might say, universally);
- whether to provide the product of service in one or more of its possible variations.

In the first case, the technological capabilities of the company remain anchored to what, in the starting up of an industry, we previously described as the original need. In the second case, on the other hand, one or more changes in the original need become what we can define as derivatives. Thus, for example, in the automotive industry, derivatives have been established over time related to automotive related sports, social status, money saving and a passion for adventure, which have made automobiles more detailed than they used to be to respond to the original need, as was the famous Model T Ford created by Henry Ford (one model for a single generic need of transport, produced from 1908 to 1927).

The path of demand segmentation, then, will lead the company to choose which and how many derivative needs should be satisfied; at the two extremes a single derived need or all identified derived needs. The greater the variation of articles produced, the more numerous the options available to the company and the more complex the competitive relationships, as will be discussed in this chapter. The change from the original need to derivative needs always involves a manipulation of the full range of integrated activities attributed to supply and thus to the underlying reasons for buying (Abell 1980).

In many areas, especially in so-called advanced economies, the original functions of use have often lost their importance; evolution, that is, changes in consumers' needs (induced by the same technological evolution of supply), has effectively imposed a general shift from the original need to more specific and sophisticated needs in a growing number of technology areas. In other cases the process of products segmentation does not begin, either because the original need is substantially effective in guiding supply or because it evolves over time without requiring variations of products. For many years, Microsoft was able to satisfy the need for a universal-type operating system (DOS-Windows) without any significant changes to the type of article supplied.

As will be seen in the section on analysis, it is not easy to unravel the tangle of needs because the ways in which needs and technologies meet is becoming increasingly complex and unpredictable. For example, today the purchase of electric cars has been rated as one of the many needs that characterize the derivative needs of the automotive industry. According to some analysts, the time is ripe to further differentiate the need for electric vehicles. In a report recently published by a North American consulting firm, the following are identified as different areas (corresponding to the derivative needs):

- driving around town (about 700 short trips per year, 9,000 miles a year and an average of 13 miles per trip);
- delivery (about 500 trips a year, 12,000 miles a year, for an average of 24 miles per trip);
- commuting (15- or more-mile trips from home to the workplace on a regular basis at a speed close to highway limits, 450 trips a year for a total of 15,000 miles, for an average of 33 miles per trip);
- driving by a typical sales rep (many long distance trips, approximately 600 trips a year for a total of 25,000 miles per year with an average of 42-mile trips).

THE GEOGRAPHICAL DESTINATION OF SUPPLY AND THE STRATEGIC SCOPE

The second dimension of positioning is the geographical area of operation and thus the choice of the geographical location for supply. Combined with segmentation it gives rise to the strategic scope. Generally, the choices you can make along the spatial dimension of positioning are of three types:

- local positioning (which may, for convenience of presentation, coincide with the nation);
- multi-local positioning, which includes presence in several countries;
- global positioning, which overcomes the multi-area in favor of a global presence (wherever possible).

The geographic location together with the segmentation of needs define the potential size of the supply area, namely the strategic scope; their joint action gives rise to the size of markets and more generally to 'scope'. If, besides satisfying needs we also consider their degree of quantitative significance (for instance, how many customers are involved), the picture is complete. We can claim therefore that:

$$S_0 = \sum_{i=1}^{N} B_i \times R_i \times RG_i$$

S_0 is the strategic scope at time t_0 given by the sum 1 to N of the satisfied needs (B) for their quantitative significance (R), and for the range of geographical penetration (RG). The scope can be broad or narrow according to the range of action of each of the three factors.

When the business is positioned with no segmentation, and thus only meets an original need, the extension of the supply will depend only on the geographical extent (given the nature of the need), which can vary between a local, multi-area or global positioning. In cases where the company has segmented on the basic need, then the extension must be read by combining the 'what' (number of derivative needs satisfied) with the 'where'.

DISTINCTIVENESS

The third and last area of positioning is the type of distinction that the company intends to pursue to meet the need. Companies seek distinctiveness in two directions: the value that the purchaser gets and the cost of production. In the first case, the company differentiates its supply from the competition and thus offers a product or a service whose value is perceived to be greater. In the second case, the cost of production-distinctiveness is pursued through the efficiency of production processes. Even in this case it is possible to rank the performance of various businesses, based on the total cost of producing one product unit (or service). On a theoretical level, the choice of distinctiveness consists in positioning the supply in relation to these areas of reference. In fact, operationally speaking, the company can decide to do the following for any identified need:

- to pursue distinctiveness based on the value generated for the customer; this is positioning based on supply differentiation;
- to pursue distinctiveness through efficient production, and therefore through production costs; in this case it is positioning based on an efficient production/distribution process;
- to pursue both types of distinctiveness;
- not to pursue any type of distinction, but to maintain or achieve a balanced position.

The choice of positioning without distinctiveness is not surprising; it is indeed a plausible option when:

- the current competitive position does not allow the company to pursue goals of distinctiveness, at least for a certain period of time, in which case it is a conservative choice, pending on change in competitive conditions;
- the current structural conditions of the competition do not allow any competitor to position themselves in a distinctive way (conditions are close to perfect competition).

THE CONFIGURATION OF THE COMPETITIVE PROCESSES

The processes are a coordinated set of homogeneous operations or activities, whose logic of aggregation depends on the nature of the final output. From a strategy standpoint, it is important to understand whether their configuration (which we call 'competitive') is consistent with the other components of the competitive structure. For example, the choice made by Apple years ago (2001) to open their own stores (Apple Store) in addition to online sales and traditional authorized dealers was the result of competitive positioning in which the segmentation of satisfied needs grew and with them the solutions (products/services) offered.

The competitive configuration of processes concerns the structure of the adopted macro business activities and key policies. The structure of macro activities refers to both the nature of the main business activities and their extension. The main business activities are:

- transformation, to be understood in a broad sense, that is also inclusive of services and farming;
- processing activities downstream of marketing activities;
- upstream of processing activities, interface activities with resource markets, type of materials, intellectual and financial (including human resources) necessary to carry out activities.

To understand the nature of macro activities, we must analyze the main criteria by which they are performed in the company (which solutions are adopted, with which knowledge, with which reference culture, etc.), at times regardless of the organizational forms formally employed. It is also very important to analyze the relationships between one macro activity and another. The extent of a business's main activities, an aspect in a certain quantitative sense of the configuration process, however, depends on:

- the level of vertical integration along the specific value chain, including choices on product distribution;
- making or buying choices, but not limited to the phenomenon of vertical integration, but more generally applied to any activity;
- production/logistics and commercial localization (how many and where).

In recent years, decisions aimed at the rationalization of the so-called supply chain, for example, the production chain that accompanies the transformation of raw materials into a finished sold product through various stages of production, have become of strategic value, meaning they are found to be a major cause of the competitive success or failure of individual businesses positioned along the chain. The phenomenon becomes even more important and complex by the increasing globalization of these chains; the production history of many products seems to be a detailed trip around the world.

The global integration of production chains is so significant as to influence the nature of relations between countries (just think of the complex web of corporate and currency interests that currently characterize the relationship between the United States and China) or to modify the role that a national business can have in an entire production industry. The leather industry, for example, is characterized by a highly globalized chain, in which Italian producers have had to manage relationships with raw material (hides) suppliers upstream, occasionally becoming partners with them in their countries (Brazil in particular) and, downstream relationships with customers, choosing to relocate production (e.g., in China for furniture and automotive industries), imposing *follow the client* type behavior.

As a consequence, it brings us to the policies adopted by a company, designed as a set of rules of conduct to guide the decision making according to a certain logic. More precisely, policies have two main functions (O'Shaughnessy 1995 , Beretta Zanoni 1997):

- they consistently and systematically guide (as opposed to overriding goals) the decisions of the various players who have decision-making responsibilities;
- they define a standardized behavioral practice.

The criterion used to identify policies should be as consistent as possible with the business industry structure. Thus, it is also possible, as is found not by chance, in various strategic analysis papers, to classify the policies using a combination of typically functional and procedural criteria. For example, the strategically relevant policies according to Hax and Majluf (1995) are:

- financing
- human resources
- technology
- supply
- production
- marketing

Horizontal synergies, because they affect both policies and the configuration of macro activities, deserve a separate observation. In fact, the presence in several competitive arenas, with or without technological diversification, allows certain conditions to achieve horizontal synergies, which can occur as economies of the competitive scope or synergies of differentiation. The first, economies of competitive scope, consist of creating a supply system which, under equal conditions, has a lower unit cost than it would have without synergies. The second, synergy of differentiation, allows the perceived quality of the goods or services to be improved.

It is hardly necessary to point out that the exploitation of these synergies requires a specific design of business processes, namely macro activities and policies. For example, an activity that you believe should be carried out in outsourcing in the case of a focused firm may instead be internalized in the case of a diversified company.

THE COMPETITIVE ARENAS

Among the results that characterize a competitive structure, the first to be considered is the competitive arena, which can be defined as:

- the set of firms competing to meet a need, whether original or derivative;
- the set of relationships that arise between competitors and between competitors and other players (such as suppliers) and that are important to the development of competitive dynamics.

The result is a competitive arena, because it forms in relation to the positioning choices made by various competitors. But how similar should two positions be to actually give rise to competition? And how can we assess the degree of similarity and intensity?

To answer this, we must proceed in steps. First, it must be determined whether the satisfied need, or group of needs, is effectively satisfied by other players. In essence, positioning on the same needs is a necessary condition in order to identify a competitive arena. Competitors can reach these needs by different paths (no segmentation, segmentation, segmentation in one way rather than another). However, what matters is to understand how and to what extent competitors overlap—completely or partially.

A second step consists in verifying whether companies that are overlapping in terms of functions of use also overlap from the localization and range of action standpoints. Again, we may have fully overlapped companies (local competitors) or partially overlapping companies (for example, local competitors competing with multinational competitors). Or a company that operates on a national market may face various types of competitors, namely:

- those operating within the same national borders;

- those operating in a subset of the relevant geographic area, such as one or more regions;
- those operating in a wider geographical area (continental or global) and for which therefore the geographical scope of analysis is only a subset of its geographical positioning.

The third step should focus on assessing the position of businesses in terms of what type of distinctiveness they seek. Because there is more than one possibility in this case (no distinctiveness, distinctiveness on the cost side or differentiation side or both), there can be various levels of overlap (full or partial). Moreover, the distinctiveness overlap should be assessed very carefully because the lack of overlap does not necessarily imply the absence of competition. In some cases, companies that are cost-positioned may not compete with those who are positioned on differentiation, whereas in other cases they would.

This analysis of the three areas of positioning should lead to two conclusions:

1. it is necessary to identify what might be called the limit of positioning overlap, namely that minimum degree of overlap below which a competitive relationship cannot be identified. The limit of overlapping substantially signals the extension of the competitive arena and its borders;
2. within these borders, thus above the limit of overlap, the identified competitors do not all have the same ratio of competition. In other words, some competitors have very similar positions and others, while being above the limit, are more distant. We shall call the former primary competitors and the latter secondary competitors. Note that the techniques used for analysis of strategic groups (pure and hybrid) can also be used to distinguish primary competitors from secondary competitors.

Another element we need to take into consideration is the technological paradigm used by competitors, whether they are primary or secondary. We have already had occasion to recall that competitors normally operate in the same industry and thus use the same production technology. However, this coincidence cannot be taken for granted; different technologies can be used to satisfy the same need. It is therefore necessary to know what the technological paradigm of reference is for each competitor; this means not only verifying industry membership, but more generally examining the overall system of knowledge that the competitors have or are developing.

Whereas the distinction between primary and secondary competitors allows us to assess the degree of homogeneity in the different positions, this second distinction makes it possible to assess the degree of technological homogeneity of competitors. Competition with technological heterogeneity

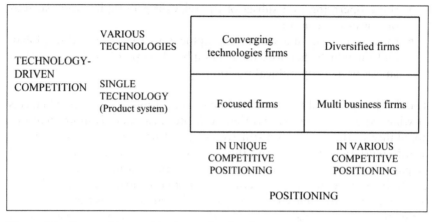

Figure 4.3   Competitive positioning and technology.

is often very insidious because it can introduce significant discontinuities in the competitive balance and because it generates competitive phenomena that are not easy to interpret (Bower and Christensen 1995, Christensen 1997). By distinguishing the competitive arena from the industry, we can affirm that not only are there *multi-businesses* that operate in multiple industries (thus having several productive technologies or product/service systems) but there are also those with a single production system in several competitive arenas. Figure 4.3 allows us to identify some typical situations:

- focused businesses, namely with a single technology present in a single competitive arena;
- companies with converging technologies, which are present in a single competitive arena but which apply various types of technology (product systems) to meet demand;
- *multi-businesses*, present in several competitive arenas using a single technology (product system);
- diversified companies, which combine various technologies with presence in different competitive arenas.

CRITICAL FACTORS AND FACTORS OF RELATIVE STRENGTHS AND WEAKNESSES

Because the competitive arena is a set of relationships between competitors and other economic players, it can be described by the critical factors that characterize it together with the factors of strength and relative weakness of a company (or rather, of each competitor). With the term critical factors we mean those specific characteristics of supply and the production process that are particularly instrumental in satisfying a need and thus in conquering the market. For example, for certain products delivery time can be a critical factor, for others a critical factor would concern sale prices (and therefore the cost of production), and for others the brand, and so on.

The industry structure certainly has some importance in determining the critical factors of a competitive arena; however, because the industry (understood in the technological sense) is only one component in the competitive arena, the critical factors are generated also by other causes, particularly by how the different positions overlap, forming the competitive arena. Critical factors can be linked to the strengths and weaknesses of each competitor. The factors of strength and relative weakness are competitive abilities, higher or lower, respectively, than those attributable to direct competitors, whether primary or secondary, based on the critical factors identified. Overall, they should help to identify the source of competitive differences. Continuing in the example, if a critical factor is the product delivery time, then the quality of the logistics process becomes a factor of strength or weakness, depending on whether it is relatively high or low.

The idea that every company has strengths and weaknesses is simple and perhaps for this very reason it is commonly used in the strategic field, as it was in the first considerations in the 1960s with SWOT analysis (Andrew et al. 1965) or in the 1970s with the PIMS program (Profit Impact of Market Strategies) (Buzzell and Gale 1987). Like all simple concepts, however, this one clearly shows a degree of fragility if interpreted incorrectly. For example, what constituted a strength can turn into a weakness in just a few years (more rarely the opposite), causing a crisis for the companies that were held as examples of excellence only a short time before. The fact is that the factors of strength and weakness only make sense if placed in relation to critical factors, but they themselves are critical factors only in relation to contingent competitive forms. For this reason, both critical factors and the factors of strength and weakness can change rapidly and confuse those who had interpreted them broadly or, worse, taken them to be the rule.

In short, thinking in terms of critical factors and factors of strength and relative weakness has only one purpose: to simplify and speed up the understanding of what is currently happening in a given competitive arena.

THE RESULTING COMPETITIVE POSITION

The resulting competitive position indicates in a given time what the relationship is between the company and its direct competitors (and thus, for each competitive arena). In particular, a company has a competitive advantage when the difference between the value generated for the customer (that is, the net benefit obtained from purchasing the product and service) and costs incurred by the company is greater than that which usually characterizes the competitors' supply system. Basically, the competitive position may be one of the following types:

- at an advantage, by leveraging the 'value for the customer' dimension, the 'production costs' dimension, or both (similar to what has already been seen in the choice of positioning in the distinctiveness dimension);
- in a state of equilibrium;
- at a disadvantage, to the extent that others benefit from the value and/or cost dimensions.

In a dynamic sense, it is usual to identify a position of advantage (for costs or differentiation) even when, besides its current position, a company demonstrates a clear potential to increase the value generated for the customer more proportionately to an increase in production costs or, conversely, to reduce costs without greatly affecting the value. This is a condition that, more or less rapidly, will result in a favorable position.

The cause-effect relationship between factors of strengths/weaknesses and competitive position is very strong. Intuitively a company that has many strengths and few weaknesses is likely to have a competitive position of advantage; the reverse will apply for a business with many competitive weaknesses and few strength factors. However, the relationship among weaknesses, strengths and competitive outcome depends on:

- how various factors of strength and weakness blend; for example, a single factor of weakness in some cases may undermine the positive effects of all factors of strength;
- the choice of positioning, which could, for example, be wrong despite the factors of strength and weakness;
- exogenous phenomena, which often act in an unpredictable manner and in a context of random ambiguity.

One aspect to consider is the role that price plays compared to competitive position. The price of supply is not, in and of itself, a decisive element in assessing the competitive position. Rather, if a company has an advantage, the variable prices will determine to what extent the consequent benefits can be had. We consider that (Hoopes et al. 2003):

- the purchaser acquires a good or a service at a specified price (P) in order to obtain a certain benefit (V);
- the company produces and sells the good or service at a specified price (P), claiming a certain level of costs (C).

The surplus value obtained by the buyer is the difference between the value of supply (V) and price (P), whereas surplus for the producer is the difference between the price (P) and cost (C). The cost advantage allows a maximization of the margin per unit (P-C) or a maximization of sales volume with the same margin (or both possibilities). The advantage of differentiation, instead, leverages on a maximization of V, at least potentially resulting in a rise in P (premium price), or an increase in sales volumes (or, in this case, some combination of the two possibilities). Naturally, the greater the competitive advantage, that is, the difference between the benefit conferred to purchaser and the cost of production, the greater the leeway available to the company in setting their pricing policy.

We come now to the relationship between competitive advantage and economic performance (profitability). In the past, many authors have substantially equated the two results by defining advantage as the achievement of over-performance (Grant 1988). It was an understandable choice, if only because the strategic behavior physicologically tends to the creation of over-performance (Scott Morton 2000). Nevertheless, competitive position and income performance are two different phenomena albeit obviously related. To begin with, we have defined the competitive advantage based on the difference between value and cost, where value refers to the buyer's degree of appreciation of the supply but not price. So it is clear that advantage and performance are placed on two different levels, one could say by definition, in the sense that the first concerns a strong ability to generate value over the competition, whereas the second concerns the method and timing with which the company can or will gain this value (Newbert 2008). But even switching from value to price, the relationship between competitive position and over-performance should not be taken for granted (Baaij et al. 2004). On a logical level, we should ask ourselves whether it is also true that the presence of a competitive advantage is both a necessary and sufficient condition for the achievement of economic profit, or if, on the contrary, it can be achieved in the absence of competitive advantages, or whether competitive advantages can be achieved without financial gain.

On this subject, the literature has shown that there are many external factors to business that affect the ability to generate income over a long period (positively or negatively), thus regardless of the competitive positions reached (Newbert 2008). On closer inspection, the phenomenon is attributable to an aspect of the competitive dynamics already addressed; the source of business profits lies not only in terms of the single unit (company), which is the level of its competitive advantage, but also at different levels, such as business objectives, be they industries, competitive arenas, strategic groups or any other form of aggregation (Ketchen and Shook 1996).

In short, the presence of structural phenomena, plus the role of the corporate level in companies in several arenas, allows us to conclude that a position of competitive advantage is neither a necessary nor sufficient condition in the achievement of economic profit. It is not a necessary condition because the mere presence in certain industries can ensure an 'average' company a structural income. Nor is it a sufficient condition because in an industry where income is structurally lower than the cost of capital invested, any benefit would be useless on the income level (at least for a certain period of time).

5 Scenario Analysis

The scenario analysis focuses mainly on four areas:

- the 'embryonic' competitive vision;
- the current competitive structure;
- the general scenario;
- the industry scenario.

ANALYSIS OF THE 'EMBRYONIC' COMPETITIVE VISION

The 'embryonic' competitive vision is an early form of strategic vision and is the result of past experience, organizational ideologies and the beliefs of individual managers. It is not based on an analytical path but advances indirectly towards strategic behavior (Normann 1977).

Typical questions that this phase of the analysis attempts to answer are as follows.

- Is there a competitive view of an embryonic type, and if so, what is its nature?
- How was it formed and when? What events and experiences can it be traced back to?
- What is relevant in determining the analytical process first and strategic decisions second?

There are two particular objectives of the analysis: understanding the nature and origin of the embryonic competitive vision and the degree of influence it exerts on decision-making.

With regards to the source, three factors are relevant.

1. Basic cultural orientation (Coda 1988)—namely that complex set of values rooted in the key players (core ideology) in relation to the role and purpose attributed to the company (emphasis on profit, growth orientation, nature of the relationship with stakeholders, etc.), the scope of company operations (diversified, focused, with a vocation to the financial rather than production, etc.), the management

philosophy and organizational reference (leadership style, organizational culture, etc.)

2. An implicit vision of the future—again, a set of beliefs on just how that future will be (not just the company) and how you would like it to be. It is an implicit vision because it is of a pre-analytical type, often unexpressed and not necessarily shared on the organizational level (in the sense that several key players can also have differing implicit visions).

3. A competitive philosophy—that is, a rough guide on how you would govern the competition (aggressively or conservatively, focusing on a country or dealing with globalization, opening or closing to a network of relationships, with a propensity or aversion to financial and operational risks, etc.).

It is then necessary to assess the degree of influence that the embryonic vision actually has on decision makers. The significance of an embryonic competitive vision varies depending on the organizational context. In particular, the link between the embryonic competitive vision and strategic choices is mediated by the analytical process; that mediation will be more or less relevant, depending on the quality of strategic analysis (its effectiveness) and depending on the confidence that management feeds into it (which depends on cultural aspects).

We see the two extremes and opposing positions. Wherever the process of strategic analysis is well structured and widely used by decision makers in developing the strategic plan, the embryonic competitive vision essentially indicates the direction that the analytical path should follow. And this is not negligible. Like all learning processes, strategic analysis is not neutral because it depends on instruments of a technical nature. However, if the analytical process is not technically sound or not culturally supported, then it will not affect the content of strategic choices and the embryonic competitive vision will prove to be decisive.

ANALYSIS OF THE CURRENT COMPETITIVE STRUCTURE

After understanding the nature and origin of the embryonic competitive vision, we can check to see what the competitive structure of a company is and, in particular, the degree of coherence that binds the different elements.

Basically, the questions that characterize this first level step are the following:

- what aspect did the competitive structure have in the past and how has it changed over time to date?
- is the current competitive structure internally consistent? Are there any features of inconsistency? Which ones and why?

- is the current competitive structure consistent and functional to the embryonic competitive vision?

The competitive structure is a complex structure, where individual elements interact dynamically with each other. There is no doubt that structural consistency should be evaluated at both global and unitary levels. Nevertheless, the task can still be simplified by taking some partial steps.

The consistency between the need met, the distinctiveness chosen and the geographical range of action must be evaluated for each competitive position. This can be further enhanced by a joint analysis of the identity of the buyers and the nature of the product used (Figure 5.2).

For each position the perimeter of the competitive space of reference must be defined through the identification of the different positions on the market and the resulting overlapping areas. After defining the space, it is relatively easy to determine the critical factors, the relevant strengths and weaknesses and the competitive position achieved. In this phase, where the goal consists mainly in an assessment of overall consistency of the current system, it is essential to understand if the positioning choices have actually led to the competitive outcomes sought (Figure 5.3). For example, if the company chose differentiation, was the competitive outcome actually achieved? Based on which strengths and weaknesses?

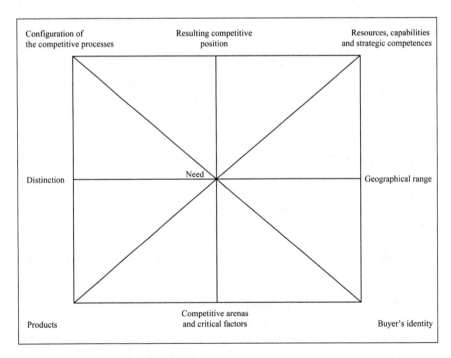

Figure 5.1   The competitive structure.

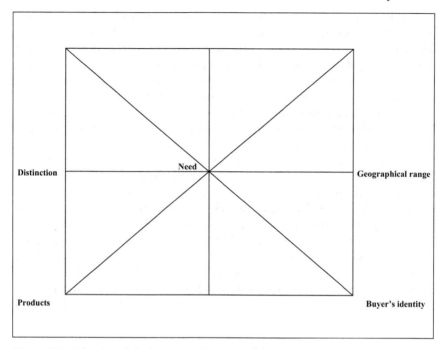

Figure 5.2   Identity of the buyers and nature of the product.

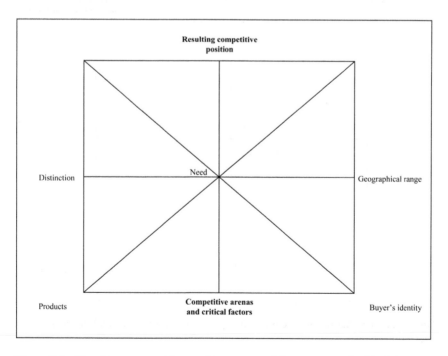

Figure 5.3   Resulting competitive position, competitive arenas and critical factors.

The last step is to assess the consistency between the elements of the competitive structure seen so far and the competitive configuration of business processes as well as of the available resources (i.e., the combinations of resources, capabilities and strategic competencies). Given a certain range, which in turn is the result of a certain positioning, how consistent are the configuration of competitive processes and available resources (Figure 5.4)?

In 2006, Nintendo launched motion gaming with the Wii and Wii-Mote consoles. With this new technology it met a need that had been unmet by video game manufacturers: the 'social' or family video game (also called 'casual gaming') that can be played together (friends, parents, children). Sony, manufacturer of the rival PlayStation, noticed over the next few years an inconsistency in its competitive structure regarding the needs that it intended to meet, which included motion gaming and its technology (products), which did not include motion gaming. In March of 2010 Sony introduced PlayStation Move with the wireless Move control, which was similar, though more sophisticated, to the Nintendo Wii Mote. More or less at the same time, Microsoft developed the Natal device for its Xbox 360 (available for Christmas 2010). In this case the motion effect is provided by a camera that records the player's movements, making him interact with the game.

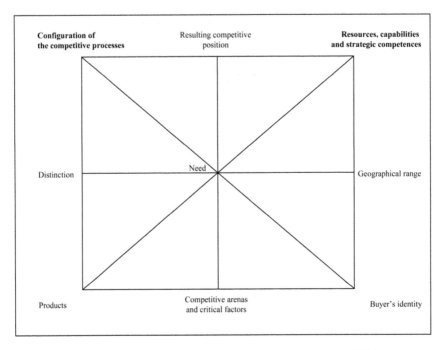

Figure 5.4 Configuration of competitive processes, resources, capabilities and strategic competences.

SCENARIO ANALYSIS

Continuous monitoring of the overall picture, or macro context, is a typical activity of strategic analysis. Macro context means the set of phenomena which, while relevant to the firm's activities (especially on a prospective basis), are not directly attributable to the typical dynamics of the industry and competitive arenas (which will be analyzed specifically). Basically, this phase of the analysis will answer two questions:

- are there trends (social, cultural, political, institutional, etc.) that may represent growth opportunities or otherwise support the strategic design process?
- on the contrary, are there trends that may pose a real threat to the sustainability of the current competitive structure or of the competitive structure that the company intends to achieve?

For some analysts, for example, the so-called 'space revolution', a concept conceived in the world of politics that has taken on a certain importance in recent years, refers to a new structure of political and economic space, where substantially every part of the planet is somehow connected to every other part, and where anything can happen anywhere and at any time (there can be innovation anywhere, anyone can be a manufacturer, anyone a purchaser, etc.). The phenomenon is complex and becomes more or less relevant, depending on the case. But the critical point is this: what in the general scenario is relevant to the individual company?

Finding an answer means on a technical level to decide what the scope of an analysis should be. In fact, a definition of the scope lies in choosing what to focus on and what to exclude; it is a difficult choice and one that always carries a high risk.

An initial determination of the objectives of a scenario analysis can contribute to a correct recognition of the scope of the analysis. For example, if the company wanted to understand whether there are any contextual conditions for an expansion of their range, then they should identify those phenomena (even seemingly distant) to which they should link their growth trend, in terms of cause and effect. For example, for the design and installation of aluminum extrusion plants, the expected developments in the construction business are key indicators towards understanding growth potential. In turn, forecasts in the construction field are based on indicators of political, economic and social nature that are fairly easy to spot. However, the scope of the analysis will be more or less broad depending on how many phenomena will be considered, the geographic area and the time frame.

The phenomena to be potentially analyzed are divided into four main areas:

1. economic in the strict sense
2. social
3. technological
4. political

Economic phenomena, for example, are GNP growth, the level of monetary liquidity in the system, access to large retailers, the level of unemployment, inflation, oil prices, interest rates and so on; in the social field we have the birth rate, family structure, level of education, the percentage of population under the age of twenty-five, etc. Technology phenomena concern investigating the activities of major research centers or investments allocated by governments in different areas of technology; and relevant political aspects regard for instance legislative activities or the campaign programs of the various political factions.

In addition to the object you must also choose the geographic scope of an analysis which, moreover, can also differ according to each specific context. For example, economic, social and political analyses might refer, say, to Europe as the geographical range, whereas technological analysis might consider the whole world. Or, for example, an analysis of interest rates might concern the whole world, whereas unemployment might concern Europe alone.

In some cases, the combination of subject and geographical area leads one to actually focus on specific geographical areas. For example, Turkey has proved to be an interesting country in the pharmaceutical industry, both as a market and as a manufacturing hub. In the period 2003–2007, pharmaceutical imports grew on average by 58% while exports of pharmaceutical products grew by 70%. And not coincidentally, a Pfizer research center opened in 2010 in Ankara at the University of Hacettepe.

Finally, to properly define the scope of scenario analysis we must also identify the time frame of reference—namely, how many years the forecast will include (the future), but also how many years data collection refers to (the past).

The resulting broadness of the scope of analysis will of course differ greatly from company to company and will tend to change over time for the same company, depending on strategic choices made or global events. The choice of scope leads us from general questions to more specific questions, more instrumental than the first. For example:

- How has the population's propensity to consume evolved and how will it evolve?
- What will happen to the anti-trust legislation in a particular country?
- What will be the trend in copper prices?
- How long will it take for basic research in oncology to get certain pharmaceutical products on the market?

INDUSTRY SCENARIO ANALYSIS

The industry scenario is the coherent representation of the future and possible structure of an industry, starting from the current structure.

Key questions that characterize a strategic analysis in this step are the following:

- What is the structure of the industry or industries in which the company operates? How has it changed over time and how could it change? What impact does the structure of an industry have on the degree of strategic discretion and on income results?
- How do reference production technologies evolve? And to what degree do my technological skills compare with my competitors?

The areas the attention is focused on are those that are important for the company, either because they already exist or because the company is in the process of assessing an entrance.

Because the number of variables that come into play can be high, a distinction must be made between independent structural variables and dependent structural variables (Porter 1985). The former, the independent variables, are elements of the structure whose future performance is not dependent on other structural elements. The latter, or dependent variables, are wholly or largely determined by other structural variables (whether they are in turn dependent or independent). The development of industry scenarios is based on the expected behavior of the independent variables, whereas the trend of the dependent variables will enter as a result (and consistently) within each scenario.

Given the distinction between the industry and its competitive space, and the technological significance given to the industry, we believe it is more effective to divide structural variables into technological variables and industrial economic variables (all others). This way, the industry scenario can be constructed by following these steps:

1. identification of the most significant technological determinants;
2. hypotheses on the possible evolutionary paths of these variables;
3. for each path/scenario, verification of the behavior of the main industrial economic determinants;
4. for each path/scenario, validation of the opportunities, given the current competitive structure (projected into the future);
5. for each path/scenario, validation of the degree of risk associated with the current competitive structure (projected into the future);
6. for each path/scenario, validation of the degree of strategic freedom and Industrial Value Asset (IVA).

Taking into account this course, it is then appropriate to consider the following:

- the technological structural determinants (or technology drivers);
- the industrial economic structural determinants (or industrial economic drivers);
- the impact of the determinants in terms of strategic freedom and Industrial Value Asset (IVA).

TECHNOLOGICAL DRIVERS

It has been said many times that an industry is a technological paradigm and for this reason technology is the determining factor in the definition of a structure. In many cases it is useful to distinguish between core technology based on fundamental knowledge that is necessary to govern the production process, and therefore the preparation of products and services, and a set of satellite technologies. The latter are represented, in higher or lower numbers, depending on the circumstances, by the technological support necessary to adjust the basic production process.

In the automotive industry, for example, due to the complexity of the basic product, there are numerous satellite technologies employed, some of which are quite sophisticated. For obvious reasons, the rate of change in satellite technology is much more intense than it is in basic technology. Moreover, the satellite technology system may play a significant role:

- in ensuring distinctiveness to some firms, when these technologies significantly determine the value of the offer and the extent of costs, and when they present greater innovative potentials compared to core technology (which as said is still generally more stable);
- in introducing innovations to core technology, when integration with it or with other technologies will significantly determine a change.

For the purposes of structural analysis, there are some features of technology (basic and satellite) that should be considered carefully. These characteristics, which can be defined as technology drivers, are the following:

- technological complexity
- rate of change in technology
- production scale
- life cycle of technology

THE COMPLEXITY OF TECHNOLOGY

Some areas require the knowledge of very sophisticated and not very accessible technology, whereas others require more modest knowledge of technology (sometimes very modest) that is easily acquired.

For some productive technological paradigms the phenomenon of technological convergence often makes the assessment of the complexity of a production technology more ambiguous from the start. For example, in the early months of 2010, Google announced the experimental launch of a one gigabyte-per-second fiber-optic network, superseding its own technology with that which typically characterizes telecommunication companies. Even companies that manage the railway network technologically converge towards telecommunications technology; in fact, taking advantage of national fiber and copper networks, rail companies can provide Internet connections for travelers as well as become Mobile Virtual Network Operators (MVNO).

The average level of investment in research and development is an interesting indicator of (but not limited to) the technological complexity achieved in this field. Another indicator is the number and importance of patents and, more generally, the intellectual property designed to protect technological knowledge. Because the basis for the degree of reproducibility of production processes is the complexity of technology and thus also for the barriers to entry, Williams has identified three types of structures based on the complexity of technology and the resulting speed of cycle imitation (Williams 1992).

1. Industries with slow imitation cycles are characterized by more complex and difficult to replicate production and distribution technologies.
2. Industries with standard imitation cycles are based on popular production and distribution processes (land lines, credit card services, auto, etc.). In this case the technology is more easily replicable, even if the size factor normally raises the level of barriers against entry.
3. Fast imitation cycle industries, finally, use more accessible and more easily reproduced technology, thus linked to more modest barriers against entry.

RATE OF CHANGE IN TECHNOLOGY

From the technological standpoint, industry changes can be interpreted on the basis of two dimensions of analysis (Stieglitz and Klaus Heine 2007):

1. the use of new technological knowledge, or alternatively of an already existing technical production system;
2. the adoption of a new or, in alternative, an already existent supply system (product and service).

When innovation is based on existing technology and the same supply system, then we are faced with incremental innovation. On the contrary, we have radical innovations, with structural changes in the industry, when innovation uses new technology and introduces new ways to satisfy demand. When new technology does not bring about changes in the nature of a product or service, innovation is called modular (and usually covers production or distribution processes). Finally, sometimes the existing technologies bring about changes in the structure of supply, giving rise to innovations that can be defined as architectural or design innovations (Figure 5.5).

The rate of change in technology depends on the frequency and intensity of its innovations. Some technologies seem to be more inclined to change than others in terms of frequency, intensity or both. Increasingly, however, innovative phenomena are becoming significant and can be considered exogenous compared to the technological paradigm of reference.

The process of introducing disruptive technologies, described by Clayton Christensen, is an effective example (Christensen 1997). Disruptive technologies essentially meet the same needs met by the dominant technology, but with distinctive elements that regard, for example, the way they are used (often easier) or the cost of acquisition (usually lower). The process described by Christensen operates in five phases.

1. When the new technology is first introduced, it appears to be less effective than the dominant one, if only because it is younger and has not yet been fully exploited to meet the needs of the market.
2. Subsequently, the new technology begins to attract more buyers, with products and services that are either cheaper or easier than those of the dominant technology.
3. Because the new technology seems to address limited fringes of the market (deemed less profitable), competitor companies that have the dominant technology do not consider the new technology and the new entrants as a serious threat against which to react.

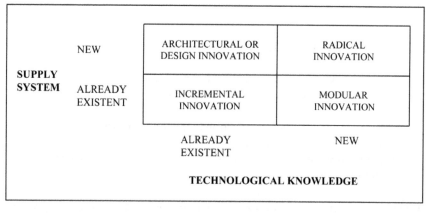

Figure 5.5   Innovation: supply system and technological knowledge.

4. And they commit a serious mistake, because at some point the new technology increasingly begins to gain more significant market share and when the threat is finally perceived seriously, it is too late.
5. The new technology completely replaces the old dominant technology and it then becomes the dominant one.

PRODUCTION SCALE

Technology also determines the minimum efficient scale of production in the industry, meaning the minimum size of the system of supply that each firm must achieve in order for the average production cost to be low enough (Collins and Montgomery 1997).

If F is fixed costs, c the variable cost per unit and q the production quantities, the total cost C is:

$$C = F + cq$$

and the average cost of production AC will be equal to:

$$AC = \frac{F}{q} + c$$

If we define c as the average cost that allows the company to operate in the field, and the minimum efficient scale q as the amount of production so that the average cost is equal to c', then we have:

$$c' = \frac{F}{q} + c$$

$$q = \frac{F}{c' - c}$$

In essence, a rise in fixed costs increases the minimum efficient scale.

In a given industry there are economies of scale (or increasing returns to scale) when the average cost decreases as production increases, and that is when average costs are greater than marginal costs. It is easy to prove that this condition occurs only when average costs decrease. The relationship between average costs and marginal costs is defined as the coefficient of economies of scale. Given the ES coefficient of economies of scale, and CM of marginal costs, we have:

$$ES = \frac{AC}{CM} = \frac{c + \dfrac{F}{q}}{c} = 1 + \frac{F}{cq}$$

Even for the ES coefficient, fixed costs are relevant. Areas where the incidence of fixed costs is greater will be characterized by greater economies of scale. The incidence and significance that fixed costs have in an industry, which is fundamental to understanding the phenomena related to the minimum efficient scale and economies of scale, in turn depend on the nature of the technology and the current stage of its life cycle.

Certain technologies, for example, require large investments in production facilities, others in research and development, others in complex distribution networks and so on. This has an impact on the structural quality and quantity of the costs that companies incur to operate in the field. Production technologies that require high fixed costs also require high volumes; only in this way the product unit cost is kept at an acceptable level compared to the value generated for the customer (and therefore compared to the sale price). Companies that work with production technologies with low fixed costs have high production flexibility because the unit cost is largely made up of variable costs.

Technology also has a direct impact on another aspect related to the scale of production: economies of experience or learning, which relate to a decrease in unit production costs as a result of an increase in cumulative production over time. According to research, the effect of experience can in some cases result in a decrease—from 10% to 30%—of unit costs for each doubling of cumulative production (Collins and Montgomery 1997).

At first, the effect of experience was attributed solely to individual knowledge. Today it is understood that the issue is more complex and involves many phenomena such as technological and organizational change (Pattinson and Teplitz 1989). However, the nature of the production process, and thus production technology, is undoubtedly at the basis of the shape (more or less inclined) that the experience curve takes. Research has shown the different effects of experience in various fields including chemical, medical and computer (Lieberman 1984, Ghemawat 1985) industries.

TECHNOLOGY MATURITY AND INDUSTRY LIFE CYCLE

Another important aspect to consider is the degree of maturity of the technology used and the industry's consequential stage of development. That the industry follows a certain life cycle, usually divided into the stages of introduction, growth, maturity, saturation and decline (S-shaped curve), is a widespread idea (Hofer 1975, Jovanovic 1982, Keppler 1997), even if the life cycle model is initially applied only to product sales (Levitt 1965, Kotler 1972).

It must also be said that the study of the life cycles of many fields has led to the identification of numerous variations outside typical performance, as regards both the duration of the stages and their very existence. For example, in some areas, defined as 'quick introduction industries', the stages of maturity and saturation are almost non-existent as we move from growth to decline. In other cases, we witness the start of a new growth cycle during a decline (areas subject to regeneration), and so on.

By focusing exclusively on technological variables we can identify two particularly significant dimensions of analysis:

1. the amount of technological knowledge accumulated (Malerba and Orsenigo 1996, Stieglitz and Heine 2007);
2. the number of companies that access the technological production paradigm (Maksimovic and Phillips 2008).

The two dimensions measure the margins of innovation and change that a particular technology has and its degree of accessibility and attractiveness, respectively. Both can be measured through a comparison between different sectors and the development of median values (i.e., number of patents registered and the number of established enterprises). Using these two dimensions, four stages in the life of a given sector can be identified.

It begins with a production technology exploration stage, in which the rate of accumulation of knowledge is still low (the reference technology model is still under development) and the number of entrants is very high (even if those entrants are often rather insignificant and short-lived).

In the expansion phase, as the technological paradigm of reference asserts itself, the rate of accumulation of technological knowledge increases, and the same applies to the number of new entrants, which is more significant at this point than during the exploration stage.

During consolidation, the rate of accumulation reaches its highest point and the number of new businesses that access this technology begins to decline.

During the decline stage, the process of accumulating technological knowledge goes down to zero, as does the number of new business entries.

THE INDUSTRIAL ECONOMIC DETERMINANTS

The industrial economic determinants are linked to technological determinants, although not necessarily in a relationship of cause and effect. Let's take a closer look at the main industrial economic drivers.

1. The average size of an industry's companies, or the number of companies and the level of concentration (for instance, measured with the four-firm concentration ratio, C4, obtained as the ratio of sales volumes of the first four companies and the sales volumes of all the firms in the industry).
2. The degree of globalization of the industry which is, in extreme cases, at the opposite end of its international fragmentation. An industry is considered to be globalized when the production technology it uses is substantially uniform worldwide. On the other hand, it is rather fragmented when, for each significant location, technological dynamics are formed which are not entirely consistent with

each other and still perhaps not yet integrated (though, of course, being part of the same area they belong to the same technological production paradigm). The automotive industry, for example, uses a global technological system where knowledge of the individual producers is similar and which follow a similar path (albeit with different results). Textiles, publishing and many service industries are generally internationally fragmented industries.

3. The degree of vertical integration, upstream and downstream, which usually characterizes an industry and which gives rise to the vertical extension of its technology, compared to an ideal supply chain that goes from raw materials to the distribution of the final product or service. By analyzing this characteristic, we can understand the degree of bargaining power attributable to buyers and suppliers.

4. The presence and resulting characteristics of a system of laws and regulations specific to an industry that can be either global or, as is most often the case, national. For example, in the railway industry, international passenger transport was liberalized in Europe in 2010 with different consequences on the competitive dynamics within each individual country and continent.

5. The structure of demand that, taken in a general sense, is a set of habits that characterize the way of acquisition of the supply system in an industry. Even the price elasticity of demand, meaning the price elasticity of the demand for a single product supplied (for example, a soft drink brand) as well as price elasticity of supply in the general sense (soft drinks) is included in the industry of demand. The Rothschild index provides a measure of the relationship between the price elasticity of a single product supplied and overall elasticity:

$$R = \frac{E_T}{E_F}$$

where:

R: Rothschild Index;

E_T : elasticity of total demand;

E_F : elasticity of individual demand (for single supply).

6. The degree of differentiation—compared to high uniformity, among the supply systems of the various industry participants (which can only be significant at the global or local level depending on the degree of globalization of the industry).

7. The technology replacement cycle—to be understood as a shift at the time of demand from one type of technology (industry) to another.

Each of the technology drivers has varying and variable degrees of impact on the economic determinants of an industry. For example, the production scale has significant effects on the average size of businesses and their numbers; the complexity of the technology often has effects on the degree of globalization of the industry or on the degree of differentiation; the rate of technological change can affect the replacement cycle; and technological maturity can affect the degree of vertical integration.

The relationship between technological determinants and industrial technological determinants has a greater impact on the gradual establishment of the technical production system.

Thus it is possible to identify at least two steps. During the exploration phase and partially during the expansion stage, the industry structure is still very fluid and variable. The duration and volatility that characterize this first step depends on several characteristics, such as the degree of innovation of the technology introduced, in particular, and the type of the companies involved (size, available resources, relationships with the financial system, strategic capabilities, etc.). During the expansion and consolidation stages, the structural dynamics tend to stabilize. The technology used, first a basic form which then becomes progressively accessorial, assumes a final form and acts increasingly more predictably on the structural characteristics of the industry. The number of new entrants and of companies leaving settles down to a physiological level, and global and local technological leadership consolidates. During decline, when the technology replacement cycle begins to accelerate, the link between drivers and structural characteristics becomes weak again, this time due to a progressive loss of the technology's economic significance.

STRATEGIC SCOPE AND THE INDUSTRIAL VALUE AREA (IVA)

The technological and industrial economic determinants generally have very significant effects on competitive dynamics. These effects are evident on at least two levels: the degree of strategic freedom of industry companies and the range of variability within which the main economic variables move.

Strategic freedom can be defined as the discretion that the industry structure leaves a firm in making its strategic choices (including competitive positioning and process configuration). The links that each single technology driver and each single structural feature have with the degree of strategic freedom are quite discernable. For example, the greater the degree of supply differentiation, or the greater the rate of change in technology, the greater the degree of strategic freedom. On the contrary, more intense industry regulation or a greater tendency toward vertical integration are often associated with lower levels of strategic autonomy.

The industry structure tends to some extent to affect the variability within which the key economic variables move.

The most significant impact is on production costs or, more precisely, on the level of average costs and the incidence of fixed costs. To a lesser degree, the sector structure has an impact on two other phenomena: the value of supply from the buyer's standpoint and the risks associated with the technological production paradigm. In these two cases, the structure is less determinant than the costs because both value and risk also depend, sometimes mostly, on the dynamics of competitive space, which, as mentioned earlier, do not necessarily coincide with the industry. In other words, having identified firms in a given sector, the variance in the value generated for the customer and in operational risks is generally higher than the average costs of production or the incidence of fixed costs.

Finally, the sector structure plays a key role in determining the time frame of the technology and thus of the product/service (in terms of the life cycle of a given technology and the replacement cycle).

On this basis, therefore, we can associate each industry with a particular Industrial Value Area (IVA), which is a quantity of value generated by businesses that use the technological production paradigm. Figure 5.6 helps to clarify the concept.

The figure shows the four main economic variables, namely the value for the customer (in this case, using a simplification, the value is the result of the multiplication of the product by the sale price and quantities sold), the time frame, production costs (costs to produce a quantity) and finally the risks involved.

Prices per quantity and time frame represent an additive area in the sense that the higher they are, the greater the IVA. Quantity costs and risks represent the subtractive area because they act in exactly the opposite way.

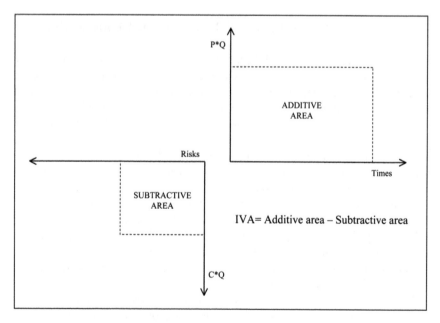

Figure 5.6 Industrial Value Area.

On a more operational level, it is possible to calculate the IVA in a given industry by determining the total value of the assets of the companies that belong to that industry. Thus, using a very general formula we can say:

$$IVA_{s,g} = \sum_{i=1}^{r} \frac{FCFO_t}{(1+WACC^*)^s} + \frac{TV_{levered}}{(1+WACC^*)^T}$$

IVA_s: industrial Value Area of industry s, in geographical area g;

$FCFO_t$:   cash flow from operations, which for simplicity we can assume to be equal to operating income after tax, of all companies operating in industry s and in the geographical area g, and generated during year t in the period from 1 to T;

$WACC^*$:   weighted average cost of capital including tax benefits derived from the financial debts of industry companies, using an industry beta and with a debt ratio on the sector's average net equity;

$TV_{levered}$:   terminal value levered, including the tax benefits derived from the financial indebtedness of industry firms.

By defining a geographical area, we can associate a final IVA that depends on the value of supply, the number of buyers, production costs, risks and the time frame of the paradigm for each sector, defined as the technological production paradigm. The value of sales and costs are aggregates that are derived from the sum of the results obtained by the companies being analyzed. The risks and time frame, on the contrary, are summary data derived from an analysis of the industry as a system (as such they are not promptly corrected data only for companies whose characteristics are median).

IVA is based on certified values and therefore the degree of technology stabilization has a significant effect not only on the size of IVA (high or low) but also on its nature. For example, in the exploration and growth stages, the expected growth in sales can be very high (additive area), but the risks may be high as well (subtractive area). The opposite may occur during the stabilization phase. Therefore, equivalent IVA can in some cases be attributed to very different structural phenomena.

6 Competitive Analysis

Competitive analysis focuses on the following areas of study:

- the available options for choosing the competitive position;
- maximizing one's competitive objectives;
- resources, capabilities, strategic competencies and processes.

ANALYSIS OF THE AVAILABLE OPTIONS
FOR CHOOSING A POSITION

The part of the analysis specifically dedicated to choosing one's position focuses mainly on the following questions:

- What are the characteristics of the competitive arenas in which a firm operates and of the competitive results obtained in each of these?
- What are the critical factors in the various arenas and the relative strengths and weaknesses of one's firm and those of its competitors?
- Will it be possible to find a new position? And how will needs/demand be met?
- Does the technology sustain and carry out the various positioning options?

To answer these questions we need to consider different elements of the competitive structure, particularly:

- the characteristics of competitive arenas;
- the competitive position obtained in each of them (including critical factors and relative strengths and weaknesses).

ANALYSIS OF THE COMPETITIVE ARENAS

An analysis of the competitive arenas must allow one to:

- correctly identify the competitive arenas and the nature of competitive relationships that exist between players;
- assess the size of the market;
- understand the nature of the competitive arenas.

Similar to what occurs with strategic grouping and in strategic business areas, a competitive arena is formed as a consequence of the positions chosen by individual companies; in other words, this space originates from an overlapping of competitive positioning. That is why relationships between rival companies can be of variable intensity according to how overlapped the positions are.

Finding the perimeter of a competitive arena requires a gradual analysis.

First of all, it is necessary to find out if the needs a firm meets are also met by other companies, and to what extent; overlapping of various intensity can be assessed (from low to high rates).

A second step consists in verifying whether the companies that overlap in terms of functions also overlap for localization and range of operations' viewpoints. In this case as well we can find real situations that are totally (for instance local competitors) or partially coincident (for instance local competitors with multinational competitors).

The third step involves the position of a firm in terms of its chosen distinctiveness.

Because in this case, too, there is more than one possibility (no distinctiveness, distinctiveness regarding costs or differentiation or both), there can be overlapping of different degrees (full or partial). An assessment of the overlapping of distinctiveness must be done very carefully because the absence of overlap in this case does not necessarily mean the absence of competition. In certain cases those who choose a position based on costs do not compete with those who have a position based on differentiation, whereas in other cases that might not be true.

The fourth step involves the technological paradigm used by one's competitors, whether they be of the primary or secondary type. Because not all competing companies use the same production technology, it is necessary to verify which technology each rival firm uses. Rival companies with dissimilar technologies are often quite insidious because they can introduce significant discontinuity in the competitive balance and because they generate competitive phenomena that are not easy to interpret (Bower and Christensen 1995, Christensen 1997).

This analysis should soon lead us to the following conclusions (Figure 6.1).

We need to find what we could call the limits of position overlapping, namely that minimum degree of overlap below which we could not find any competitive relationship. The degree of overlap basically marks the extent of the competitive arena and its perimeter.

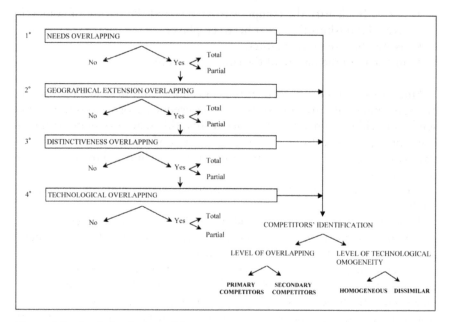

Figure 6.1   Analysis of competitive arena.

The companies identified within this perimeter, which is above the limits of overlap, do not all share the same relationships of competition. In other words, rival companies will have very similar positions to others, whereas the positions of other companies, while still within the limits, will be quite distant. We will define the first primary competitors and the last secondary competitors.

Finally, each competitor will be assessed according to the technology they use to satisfy the needs of their customers (competitors who are technologically homogeneous and those that are dissimilar).

Even an assessment of the market becomes relevant. There are three measures in this case that appear to be particularly relevant.

1. The total potential market, which means the overall demand that the market or markets in a competitive arena could potentially satisfy, even from a dynamic viewpoint. For example, to identify the potential market of online poker players in a given country, you would have to first define the social-economic profile of the players and then calculate how many individuals can be included under that profile, today and in perspective.
2. The market served, compared to the total potential market, is a sub-group of the demand that one believes can be realistically satisfied under the current conditions. The market served regarding online poker players is just a part of the potential market (a part

represented by individuals who are predominantly male with a high tendency to use the web, between eighteen and thirty-two years of age, and so on). In Apple, in view of the possibilities of the potential market, set up an extension plan significantly called 'five down ninety-five to go'.

3. Finally, the market served represents a more objective measure because it refers to the total volume of transactions carried out in a market in a given moment. For example, it has been calculated that the toy market in Italy in 2009 reached a total of €1.6 million, a 5% increase over the preceding year.

For a competitive arena, as for a given industry, it is possible to introduce a clearer, more complex form of assessment. In fact, just as it is possible to calculate the Industrial Value Area (IVA) in reference to different industries present in geographic areas, using the same logic it is possible to find the Competitive Value Area (CoVA). CoVA is obtained by capitalizing the expected operative flows of the companies included in a competitive arena.

$$CoVA_s = \sum_{i=1}^{T} \frac{FCFO_t}{(1+WACC^*)^t} + \frac{TV_{levered}}{(1+WACC^*)^T}$$

$CoVA_s$:   competitive Value Area of competitive arenas;

$FCFO_t$:   cash flow generated by operations, which for the sake of simplicity we can suppose to be equal to the enterprise's income after taxation, for all the businesses operating in the competitive arena generated in the year t in the period between 1 and T;

$WACC^*$:   weighted average capital cost including any fiscal benefits derived from financial debts of the companies in the competitive arena, using reference industry beta and with a debt/average net capital ratio for the industry of reference;

$TV_{levered}$:   terminal value levered, including fiscal benefits derived from the companies' debt situation.

Compared to IVA, CoVA can be disclosed more analytically, depending on the type of competitors. In fact, the CoVA of a competitive arena can be sub-divided into:

- homogeneous primary, which includes the value of all the assets of the primary competitors that belong to the same industry of the firm being analyzed;
- dissimilar primary, which includes the value of all the assets of the primary competitors that belong to a different industry than that of the firm being analyzed;

- homogeneous secondary, which includes the value of all the assets of the secondary competitors that belong to the same industry as the enterprise being analyzed;
- dissimilar secondary, which includes the value of all the assets of secondary competitors that belong to a different industry than that of the firm being analyzed.

Finally, an analysis of the nature of competitive arenas basically means understanding the basic rules, which may change among different competitive arenas. Anyway, economic theory has elaborated several model types to represent the competitive forms; these models are traditionally applied to industries: perfect competition, monopoly, monopolistic competition and oligopoly.

To a strategic analyst, a formal representation of the different balances is not as important as the identification of certain behavior patterns, especially as concerns production and pricing. What becomes important is mostly the phenomenon of market power, or certain companies' ability to set prices much higher than their marginal costs (with obvious consequences on profits). The market power in a competitive arena is usually measured by industrial economists using Lerner's index, which is equal to (Cabral 2002):

$$L = \sum_{i=1}^{n} s_i \frac{p - CM_i}{p}$$

where s is equal to the firm's market share i (p is price and CM marginal costs).

Industrial economy, namely the so-called new empirical industrial economy, has substantially attributed market power to three factors:

1. flexibility of demand based on price
2. number of companies in an area or their concentration
3. degree of collusion

Regarding the first factor, low elasticity of demand based on price, like every other condition, tends to reinforce the market power of dominant companies.

As regards concentration, however, it has a positive relationship with market power and is substantially known from the first actions that develop within the structure-behavior-performance paradigm. In fact, concentration reduces the effect of competitive dynamics, whose inefficiency tends to increase market power. 'Concentration' is measurable just like market power and elasticity are. The coefficients Cm (e.g., C4) can be used, which are basically the sum of the market quotes of the larger companies m:

$$C = \sum_{i=1}^{m} s_i$$

The relationship between market power, elasticity and concentration can therefore be expressed by the following formula:

$$L = \frac{H}{e}$$

Finally collusion, which consists of agreements between competitors for the purpose of reinforcing the market power of the various colluded parties. Among the phenomena that can favor or enhance collusion between competitors is the quality of antitrust regulations and the type of institutions that oversee operations. But there are other phenomena of a more clearly economic origin. For example, it has been found that agreements between companies are more probable when (Cabral 2002):

- there are few companies very similar to each other in terms of resources and behavior (symmetrical firms);
- when companies that have made agreements among themselves operate in different countries (so they are more willing to share the areas where they have influence).

In other words, we can say that competition varies significantly in relation to:

- the number of competitive players (primary and secondary) present in a competitive arena and their willingness/possibility to reach agreements;
- the distribution of market shares with, at the two extremes, situations where there is strong concentration and competition for leadership or, at the other end, fragmentation and perfect competition;
- elasticity of demand based on price.

The importance of strategic planning increases wherever the number of primary competitors and the distribution of their market quotes form a situation very close to a oligopoly, in which the decisions and behavior of each competitor are evident to others and provoke consequential decisions and behavior.

The probability of finding such situations (oligopoly) is much greater whenever the competitive arena has been defined by overlapping positions. Actually, even a fragmented industry with many competitors can include larger or smaller arenas in which a low number of primary competitors are vying for the same customers with very similar positions. In fact, a situation very close to an oligopoly is generated among these competitors.

Finally, the nature of a competitive arena should be analyzed also in its broader dimension, taking into consideration the strong relationships firms have with their suppliers and clients, potential entrants and substitute offers.

ANALYSIS OF COMPETITIVE POSITIONS

It is necessary to do an analysis of the competitive positions in order to answer these questions:

- Just how important are the advantages of companies (if they have an advantage) and of their competitors?
- How long will a firm be able to maintain an advantageous position?

We have said that a firm's competitive position, in relation to its presence in a competitive arena, is measured in relation to the difference that exists between the value of demand and its cost. It is necessary to know exactly what the relationships are between the value of demand, the net benefits for the buyer, the net benefits for the manufacturer and price.

The net benefit for the buyer (BNA) is calculated by finding the difference between the value of supply (V), or the gross benefit, and the corresponding price of the purchase (P):

$$BNA = V - P$$

The gross benefit depends mainly on the buyer's satisfaction of the purchase made, net of any costs that the buyer will have in order to 'enjoy' the purchase (which generally concerns physical or intellectual accessibility to the product or service). The buyer's valuation:

- depends on a combination of the product's technical features and of the service and perceptive types of phenomena; the prevalence of one aspect or the other depends on the specific type of transaction;
- is of a relative kind, in that it is based on a comparison of alternative offers, something often done with the aid of inadequate information.

The basic aspect of this stage of an analysis is the identification of those features that actually determine a buyer's evaluation. For an automobile, for example, dependable features can be reliable technology, the style, active and passive safety, and the brand name, which is a complex feature because it is evocative of a diverse set of characteristics.

You could say that the relationship between value and price (V/P) is a rather efficient measure of the attractiveness of a supply system for the buyer. BNA can also be equal to 0, whenever the manufacturer decides to adapt completely to the value of supply.

The net benefit for the manufacturer (BNP), however, is calculated by finding the difference between the price and the costs required to make the specific offer available on the market C. Therefore:

$$BNP = P - C$$

Remember that whereas the amount of benefit for the manufacturer depends on the number of buyers (something we will look at more closely later on), this does not normally hold true for the buyer, unless their reasons for buying are influenced by relational type phenomena (think of social networks or the use of a single operative system for buyers of personal computers).

Adding the two types of benefits—for the manufacturer and buyer—you get the total difference of V-C:

$$BNA + BNP = V - C$$

An advantageous competitive position allows a firm to achieve higher values of this difference (V-C) compared to their competitors, and therefore allows greater margins for maneuvering in the distribution of benefits, for both the manufacturer and the buyer.

As we have seen, the strategic scope increases, depending as much on geographic range as on the product supplied. Of course, the greater the scope, the greater the possibilities to take advantage of the better competitive position sooner or later achieved.

Albeit in different ways according to the structure of demand, price functions as a regulatory mechanism; in fact, once a firm has ascertained its advantageous position, through pricing it can decide to what extent it wants to rely on significant dimensions of demand (limiting or even cancelling its premium price). Or, as an alternative, it must decide whether to set a higher premium price for a limited amount of demand.

Another rather important step in a competitive analysis is understanding how sustainable advantages can be for both a firm and its competitors. Sustainability of advantageous positions definitely depends on their duration over time. The duration, however, is an effect because an advantage can be considered sustainable when the other companies, not necessarily only the primary and secondary competitors, are not able to reproduce the system of generating value adopted by the enterprise in advantage—meaning that specific relationship between the value of supply and costs (Barney 1991). Only by assessing this difficulty in reproducing the same system can a firm arrive at sensible conclusions on the sustainability of an advantage.

A simple but rather efficient way to assess the difficulty of reproduction and thereby the sustainability of an advantage is to consider what the critical factors in the competitive arena are and what the weaknesses and strengths of each rival firm are (or at least what the strengths and weaknesses of the leading firm are).

You can find the critical factors mainly by reasoning on the principles of value and cost drivers within the competitive arena (Beretta Zanoni, Colombo 2010). Regarding the former, we should keep in mind:

- the coherence between the system of supply and the functional expectations of the buyer;
- the degree of accessibility or the pleasurable use of the product or service; for physical products you must also take into consideration the efficiency of delivery;
- personalization, or the possibility for buyers to determine their personal closeness to the supply system;
- the brand and its reputation that guarantee that a product is recognized and which reduce agency costs and purchase risks.

Of the cost drivers, important aspects concern:

- scale economies and, in a broader sense, economies of scope, or synergies that allow a firm to optimize their use of production factors (supply, logistics, research and development, etc.) and to give greater value to the brand by offering a wider range of products;
- a knowledgeable economy, or the reduction of unitary costs generated by the accumulation of expertise and knowledge;
- economies of collective resources (financial, human and material);
- degree of vertical integration and outsourcing;
- organizational procedures.

The importance of these drivers varies in relation to the nature of the different competitive arenas just as, over time, the possibility to take advantage of each of the drivers to achieve an advantageous position will vary.

Once you have analyzed the importance of the values and cost drivers, it is relatively simple to identify the critical factors, which include, for example:

- sale price
- relations with distribution channels
- punctual delivery
- prestige of brand name
- variety in one's range of products/services offered
- perceived skills and competences
- relational resources
- user friendliness

We point out here that the critical factors identified in this stage are those that typically characterize the current supply system. However, nothing is keeping a firm from seeking new critical factors, even by giving up wide-spread convictions within the competitive arena. In particular, a firm could (Chan Kim, Mauborgne 2005):

- look for new critical factors;
- reduce the protection (investments) of certain critical factors;
- increase protection of certain critical factors.

At any rate, it is possible to assess the relative strengths and weaknesses of each critical factor that characterizes each competitor enterprise; from this assessment one can create an informative picture to understand just to what extent the advantageous position, achieved or endured, is actually sustainable.

ANALYSIS TO FIND NEW POSITIONS

Undoubtedly one of the creative aspects of a strategic analysis is the search for new positions. This is an experimental phase during which the analyst tries to combine the three dimensions of positioning in a new way. Usually, the entire research project revolves around the way one can express the original need in derived needs, even if, of course, one cannot ignore the fact that new positions are achieved also from new ways of making geographic or distinctiveness choices. At times new positions are the result of a firm's need to find new uses for their products, or rather, of the technology they have access to. For example, in recent years certain tanning companies have developed new areas of supply concerning new uses for leather in home decorating (wall covering or 'tiles'). This is a new market position for tanning companies in terms of responding to a need (home decorating), geographic area served (mainly in the Middle East), and distinctiveness sought (strong differentiation).

As regards method, trying to find articles that meet the demand is based on the use of different matrixes of segmentation (namely the same ones used to identify strategic groups), with which the market becomes broken down into sub-sets, each with its own motivations and reasons for buying. There are no limits to this segmentation process, unless they are used to sustain the determined products/services. Of the dimensions most traditionally used in segmentation, we mention the following:

- differences in the types of clients/customers identified through the usual socio-demographic data (age, gender, social status, education, etc.);
- differences in proposed technological solutions;
- differences in supply chain;
- differences in the geographic areas of reference.

The actual use of these or other variables serves to find in the most accurate way the motivations behind a purchase and, therefore, the nature of the derived need that one wishes to satisfy.

Of course, the more a search for new positions drives a firm to create market niches, the more critical an assessment of market size becomes. A certain position could be so original that it becomes unique, but the demand at any rate must be sufficient for the enterprise to achieve its objectives and still make a profit (or be so in perspective).

Companies offer a variety of products for the purpose of identifying market areas, or needs, which for one reason or another have yet to be met or which have not been appropriately met. It is true that, for the reasons widely discussed in Chapter 1, competition occupies a central place in the actual concept of strategy. But managing competition does not mean looking for it at all costs; on the contrary, it means trying to avoid it as far as possible (Hamel 1998, 2000).

Satisfying market needs, therefore, consists of doing a final analysis of exactly that: not only looking for new market arenas, which for various reasons have not yet been safeguarded, but above all to find new combinations between the use of resources and the supply that would be able to out-do the currently predominant value-cost combinations and assure a relatively isolated market position. More solid and sustainable advantageous positions, in fact, will be the result of these new-found combinations.

A good example is public thermal baths, many of which today are not structured to accommodate families with children (and sometimes with dogs). It just might be that new interesting possibilities for strategic development can be found among these 'non-customers'. Of course, what we call 'non-customers', or a demand not yet met, can take on the most varied forms, so it is helpful to apply some sort of classification. For this purpose the 'non-customers', according to how far away they are from the supply system, can be summarily divided into the following categories (Chan Kim and Mauborgne 2005):

1. top level 'non-customers', who use a minimal part of the current supply and who are inclined to give it up together in search of a better solution;
2. second level 'non-customers', who do not use the current offer at all mainly because they do not agree with the features of the offer or its price, even though they may be interested;
3. third level 'non-customers', who never took the slightest interest in considering the offer, also because they know absolutely nothing about it.

Each of these groups expresses their needs in a different way, and each of them offer specific opportunities to find new products/services to meet market needs.

Another aspect to take into consideration when doing a strategic analysis directed at finding new market positions consists in verifying whether and to what extent the needs identified have a significant basis, and if they are linked to sufficiently solid and promising trends. For instance, years ago the need to get around big cities in Europe had a rather consistent influence on the choice of market positions for various manufacturers of motorbikes and motorcycles. The need for 'obligatory mobility' in Europe was associated with a few trends (all quantitatively demonstrable) such as:

- an increasing presence of women in the active population;
- development of advanced services;
- the development of flexible work schedules (part-time, atypical contracts);
- new family structures especially in larger cities (separations, singles until retirement);
- the idea that public transportation was not safe (after 9/11).

Note that identifying these trends and their relative analyses represent the most obvious link between scenario analysis, at both macro and industry levels, and a competitive analysis. On the one hand, a scenario analysis can alone be enough to suggest what paths to follow to find the right article to meet a need; on the other hand, the identified needs do require quantitative support that you would get from a scenario analysis. So it is worth it to keep repeating analysis because the different objects of a strategic analysis have circular, not linear relationships.

Finally, it might be helpful to determine whether the identified needs are sustainable not only in terms of great trends but also in terms of coherence between supply and demand. Basically, this means that the identified need corresponds on the one hand to a system of coherent, plausible services/products, given the current state and potential of production technology. To meet a need in the industry including thermal bath centers for families means first determining how many families within the chosen reference geographical area could express a need, and then find out which products and services would be characteristic of the offer in this field including other offers that would require technology that is decisively distant from traditions surrounding public thermal baths and wellness (for instance a children's playground).

ANALYSIS TO OPTIMIZE COMPETITIVE OBJECTIVES

One part of a competitive analysis that is usually considered to be quite important concerns the size of competitive objectives. In this case, the analyst intends to answer the following questions:

- How many and which positions (or needs) can a firm effectively sustain?
- For each position, what competitive results can one eventually achieve? What range of action can a firm aspire to?
- With what resulting competitive position? With what relative strengths and weaknesses?

Analyses on competitive dimensions fundamentally follow two different courses, depending on whether you are doing an assessment of a defense strategy, set up to keep the customers a firm has already acquired, of how to limit the customers you are losing (a sustainable sacrifice), or of a growth strategy set up to broaden or change the basis of your customers.

In each stage of its existence, a firm has a quantitative relationship with its customers, which can be expressed by the following equation:

$$\sum_{p=1}^{n} (q_p \times m_p)$$

where:
p: positions from 1 to n;
m: market size for each p position;
q: market share for each p in the market.

These variables allow us to easily understand what options a given enterprise has. If a firm wishes to assume a more conservative or defensive type of behavior, it:

- can defend its number of positions, or the number of needs met (p), and it can defend its market share achieved for each position (q);
- can try to resist shrinking markets in which it operates (m), even without necessarily strengthening the share it have achieved.

Similarly, but at the other extreme, in the case of firm growth, it can try to:

- increase the number of positions held (p), by either introducing new products for new needs or by extending its geographic area of operation;
- strengthen its presence in markets where it already operates (q);
- contribute to market expansion (m), even without necessarily strengthening its own market share.

As regards defense options, strategic discretion changes in relation to two situations: the origin of the crisis and a firm's capital capacity.

Capital capacity allows a firm to determine what financial margins are acceptable to confront a crisis, which requires a look at their debt/capital ratio as well as at re-sizing their net capital. The origin of the crisis determines the seriousness of the problem, which at the two extremes can involve a single firm or structurally the entire competitive system.

In Italy, for example, in 2009 satellite navigator systems (or PND, Personal Navigator Device) had a 30% decline in sales (from €290 to €207); but the market shares of the main competitors did not change significantly: the Dutch company TomTom remained market leader with a market share of 58.2%, followed by Garmin with 27% and Miro with 6.5%. Analysts found several factors at the root of the shrinking sales figures such as competition from smart-phones and at the same time a lack of additional services on the PND (through cell phone connections). Keep in mind that all the situations of inefficiency come together in times of 'individual' position crises that may not be directly linked to a position, but which have to do with—in a broader sense—the configuration of enterprise processes and resources without which the firm could not have achieved its current position. From both perspectives—defense and growth—it is necessary, in order to define competitive objectives, to assess if and to what extent all the current and potential positions are sustainable from the financial balance and economic potential points of view.

To do this, each position is assessed on the basis of two situations (Figure 6.2):

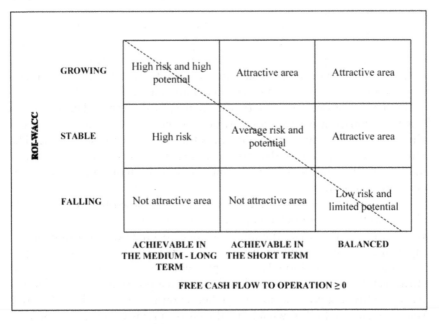

Figure 6.2 Competitive positions' assessment.

- the time it takes for incoming cash flows to at least equal outgoing cash flows (free cash flow to operation) (in the chart we hypothesize three situations: when the budget is balanced; when it will be so in the near future, when it will be so in the medium to long term);
- the difference between expected profitability from invested operative capital (ROI) to achieve a certain position and the cost of invested capital (debts plus own capital) (WACC), which can be falling, stable or growing.

The two situations allow a firm to see what the balance is among their various positions. The first, which concerns the dynamics of their operative cash flow, reveals if and when a position is at least able to finance itself and not use up the enterprise's resources. The second, which concerns profitability and the cost of capital, tells you whether a position will generate in perspective rising or falling profits. In this case, it is preferable, although more complicated, to also consider the cost of capital keeping in mind the risks of a given position and not only the amount of expected return.

The area in the bottom left (see chart), characterized by rather lengthy times to achieve financial equilibrium and by a declining ROI—WACC difference is certainly not attractive. We can say the contrary about the opposite side, in the upper right. In a general sense, we can find a line that goes from the bottom right to the upper left-hand corner, around which there are positions that are intrinsically coherent in that they match long-term achieved financial equilibrium with an important potential for compensation.

Not only the various positions should be distributed equally along the line; too many in the lower right, for example, indicates risk aversion, which also infers limited potential. On the other hand, many positions in the upper left-hand corner indicate exposure to excessive financial risk, even though it is accepted in order to find more interesting potential rewards.

Neither situation, albeit at two extremes, is desirable. The former is based on conservative positions, which do not require investments but which do not offer interesting potentials for growth at the same time. The latter is based on positions that are most likely innovative and prospectively more interesting, but which are destined to absorb financial resources over a long period of time.

The definition of competitive objectives is completed by finding targets adapted to the size of one's competitive position and relative strengths and weaknesses. In this case, the analysis done so far takes on fundamental importance in understanding exactly what size is suitable to a firm's objectives and choice of position. For example, what competitive position should a firm seek to gain a certain market share with a position based on distinctiveness? How big will the advantage be, or rather, what is the V-C ratio? And to be able to do this, what critical factors of relative strength should be developed and what weaknesses should be overcome?

ANALYSIS OF RESOURCES AND PROCESSES

As the final step in this second stage of our analysis we will consider resources and processes. There are many questions that need to be answered in this final step.

- What resources, capabilities and strategic competencies does the firm possess? How are they related to the competitive results achieved?
- Which competitive positions and objectives are actually sustainable with the current mix of resources, capabilities and competencies?
- How can new resources and capabilities be acquired, or how can the current ones be developed?
- Does the current competitive configuration of processes help to develop resources and in making position decisions?

An important primary objective of the analyst is mapping out a firm's resources, capabilities and strategic competencies. A second step is to evaluate which positions and objectives the identified resources are consistent with and with which ones they risk becoming inadequate. Later, the analyst can hypothesize on how to access new resources, capabilities and strategic competencies with the idea to broaden the strategic options that the firm has at its disposal. Then, finally, the analyst can assess what role processes should play in the competitive perspective (macro activities and policy).

MAPPING OF RESOURCES, CAPABILITIES AND COMPETENCES

To map out resources, capabilities and strategic competencies, it is necessary first of all to introduce a few hypotheses concerning the way that resources, speaking generally, become a part of enterprise processes. Originally, that is, during a enterprise's start-up phase, there are financial resources that combine with capabilities or skills. From this combination we get two different 'stocks' of resources:

- assets—tangible and intangible goods (and again financial assets);
- intangible resources.

Fundamentally, the difference between the two types lies in the fact that the goods, or assets, represent a few of the requisites that are important both as regards identification of the good itself and the possibility that it can be evaluated autonomously from any other asset the enterprise owns (Beretta Zanoni 2009).

For example, of the main international accounting standards (IAS/IFRS), the general principle used defines an asset as that firm resource from which one can rightly and specifically expect future benefits, and which is under the firm's control in that it is the firm itself that benefits exclusively from it (excluding third parties). Whereas certain intangible resources (that is, ones that are neither physical nor financial) have features like brands, patents, etc., other intangible resources, of the more organic type, do not have the same or do not yet have the same; these belong to the second 'stock' of resources that we call intangibles (or those without requisites of identification and control).

In recent years there have been numerous reports in the literature on intangible resources from which various taxonomies have arisen (Kaplan and Norton 1992, Bontis 1996, Brooking 1996, Edvinsson and Malone 1997, Sveiby 1997, McPherson 1998, Lev 1999, Lev 2002, to name a few of the more well-known). By looking at the operative notions cited in the main theories you will note that there are three vast areas for the kinds of intangible resources (and partially of intangible assets):

- human resources, or human and intellectual assets
- organizational resources—organization or structural assets
- relational resources, or resources involving relationships and reputation

Now we shall take a look at capabilities. Capabilities are divided into basic capabilities and dynamic capabilities. The former mainly involve use of those resources necessary for production and generally follow all an enterprise's activities (from logistics to production, from marketing to research and development, etc.). They can be classified on the basis of macro activities identified for the competitive configuration of processes; that is, they are those capabilities acquired in interface activities with resource markets, capabilities acquired in activities of change, and capabilities acquired in marketing activities.

The second type—or dynamic capabilities—have a different importance because, unlike the first type, they are not involved in the use of resources but in their transformation over time (Teece, Pisano, and Shuen 1997; Winter 2003; Teece 2007; Ambrosini, Bowman, and Collier 2009). Whereas basic capabilities ensure continuity of enterprise processes, dynamic capabilities generate times of discontinuity.

Dynamic capabilities, too, can be classified in various ways (Collins 1994, Winter 2003, Teece 2007, Beretta Zanoni 2008). If you think about their nature, then you can identify the following:

- learning capabilities or interpretation skills helpful in understanding certain phenomena that are important to a firm's growing competitive capabilities;
- capabilities or skills in restructuring and recombining the resources a firm owns;
- capabilities in the use of resources to develop new supply systems.

Each of these capabilities has an impact, in one way or another, on the stock of resources by changing their nature, both quantitatively and qualitatively.

For the purposes of analyzing a map of resources and capabilities, it might be more helpful to classify the dynamic capabilities according to what kind of impact they have on the stock of resources. That way we can imagine that dynamic capabilities belong to the following types (Ambrosini, Bowman and Collier 2009):

- an incremental impact on the stock of resources
- a modifying/innovative impact on the stock of resources
- a modifying/innovative impact on itself—the dynamic capabilities (also called regenerative)

Actually, a map of a firm's resources and capabilities consists of combining a firm's resources, divided into assets and intangible resources together with capabilities, both basic and dynamic, according to the impact they have on all the enterprise's resources.

Below is an example applied to a firm that offers management consulting services for which we can find combination between the more important resources and capabilities (twenty-two combinations) (Figure 6.3).

RESOURCES	BASIC CAPABILITIES			DYNAMIC CAPABILITIES		
	ACQUISITION	TRANSFORMATION	DIVESTMENT	INCREMENTAL	INNOVATIVE	REGENERATIVE
ASSETS						
FINANCIAL		Management of liquidity and short term credits		Search of new financial		
MATERIAL		External offices' management				
INTANGIBLE	Continual development of customers' database		Brand use in the selling process	Braand image and brand awareness improvement	Brand extension	
			Use of customers database	Structural development of customers' database	Development of new brands	
INTANGIBLE RESOURCES						
HUMAN	Choice of junior and senior consultants	Training of consultants			Development of new supply systems	Development of consultants' creative capabilities (not technical capabilities)
	Choice of external consultants	Projetc team management				
ORGANIZATIONAL		Identification and exploitation of procedures for the management of project team and delivery			Industrial partnership with consulting companies	Development of new delivery mechanisms
RELATIONAL	Stable relationships with customers	Customers management through the delivery process			Development of new relations management systems	

Figure 6.3   Combination between resources and capabilities.

The example helps clarify several things that we need to carry out this kind of analysis. For instance, interface capabilities with resource markets lead to the acquisition of the resources needed for a process of transformation. It should not be confused with incremental dynamic capabilities, which are geared to strengthen the resource.

In some cases, the line between them is quite subtle. In our example, the systematic creation of a customer database requires basic capabilities, whereas the structural development of the same requires dynamic capabilities (of the creative or design type). Likewise, training the consultants (above all junior consultants) from a purely technical point of view is a typical basic capability. It is a different story when trying to set up programs to develop creativity for the purpose of reinforcing a culture of innovation; in this case, your objective is not the use of a resource (through its technology), but the development of an attitude of innovation to change the capability itself (regenerative capability).

Once you have found all the different combinations of resources/capabilities that you feel are important, you can start thinking also about strategic competencies, by firstly indentifying them and then assessing their coherence with any possible strategic choices. These competencies will come from the various combinations of resources/capabilities that are particularly important to competition, at least in potential terms.

One way of finding these combinations is to evaluate the quality of resources on the one hand and the quality of capabilities on the other. High potential resources are those that are rare, valuable, impossible to imitate and suitable to production purposes.

Regarding capabilities, we can divide them into capabilities that are aligned with competition and superior capabilities (Figure 6.4). The chart shows four typical situations that correspond to the different evaluations of the resulting competencies.

The most interesting situation is the one in the upper right, where high potential resources correspond to superior capabilities. There is a very high probability that strategic competencies will be gained here.

For opposite reasons, in the lower left we can see a situation where strategic competencies will never be acquired.

In the upper left-hand corner, there are high potential resources, but they are not matched with a superior level of work or development capabilities.

In the fourth corner, superior capabilities are at work where there are low potential resources. We can say that these capabilities should be applied more efficiently.

In the chart (Figure 6.5) you can see the twenty-two different competencies found for the example of the management consulting firm.

A resource/capability/competency map is a way to do competitive self-diagnosis of the internal conditions of a firm, which becomes even more significant if associated with the main strategic choices (position, technology, competitive objectives) that the firm makes or is about to make. Of course,

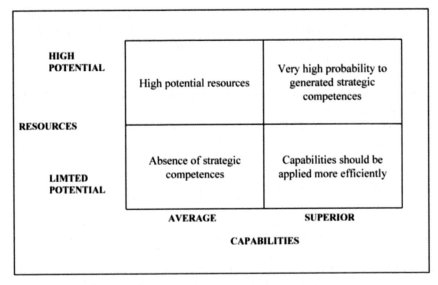

Figure 6.4   Evaluation of competences.

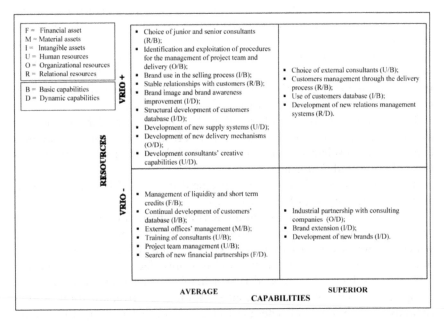

Figure 6.5   Competences of a management consulting firm.

this is a coherent assessment, but it is also an analysis of the opportunities and risks that characterize an enterprise's stock of resources. Any problems found in the analysis would require the firm to set up a realignment process with consequential:

- redefinition of the choices concerning position, technology and competitive aims;
- reconfiguration of all resources, capabilities and competencies;
- redefinition of choices and parallel reconfiguration of all resources.

ANALYSIS OF MACRO ACTIVITIES AND FIRM POLICIES

Finally, our analysis focuses on an assessment of just what structure a firm should give to its processes. The competitive configuration of processes is the way an enterprise intends to structurally achieve objectives (competitive) through the use of resources. Thereby, planning macro activities and policies means creating an organizational environment in which the firm can achieve its competitive goals.

First of all, it is worthwhile to understand the structural limitations on macro activities. The production technology utilized certainly represents a structural constraint of remarkable importance. In this regards, incidentally, the degree of vertical integration chosen by a firm plays a fundamental role in the broader process of generating value. In 2009, Oracle, the giant American software company, bought out Sun Microsystem thereby greatly expanding the area of their operations along the process of value—not only regarding software and databases, but also filing systems, server, on-line services, etc. The buy-out was the result of a radical change in Oracle's market position, which had also partly involved their competitors HP and Dell. Integration of the two companies meant that Oracle had to re-plan the overall macro activities and policies, especially the relationships with customers.

Furthermore, decision makers might be limited in re-defining policies also by reference markets. For instance, R&D market requires researchers connected with scientific communities, which have their own sets of rules (formal but mainly informal).

The same can be said about outsourcing decisions, which can be considered only if the market offers the chance.

Similar restraints can be found within a firm, in the cultural and organizational practices that characterize any kind of organization and which are not always easily or quickly modified. Of course, the analyst must point out any opportunities and not only decisional restraints. For instance, we have already said that a firm's presence in more than one competitive arena, with or without technological diversification, allows them to create horizontal synergies that can manifest as competitive economies or as differentiation synergies.

Taking advantage of horizontal synergies requires specific planning of enterprise processes on both macro activity and policy levels. For example, an activity that is considered for outsourcing in a single-product firm, could be carried out better internally in a diversified firm.

Another facet that absorbs a good part of a strategic analyst's time and attention is the alternative between growth from external activities and growth from internal activities, which is very important in the case of strategic approaches involving expansion.

Both the specific literature and practical experience have shown that both alternatives can be applied with costs, expected benefits and risks that may vary decidedly from one situation to another. It is necessary therefore to carry out an analysis:

- to try to find the best alternative between the two types of growth;
- in the case of growth from external activities, to identify possible targets and, at least on a broad scale, the basic conditions for a buy-out.

This idea can be applied in a more general sense also to alliances that can be evaluated as an alternative way to achieve one's competitive objectives, as regards growth from both external and internal activities.

7 Analysis of Impacts

The last part of the analysis focuses on the impact that strategic decisions have in terms of actions (action plan), in economic and financial terms (business plans) and in terms of outlining a strategic design with the establishment of a strategic plan.

In this final chapter we will consider:

- an analysis aimed at identifying actions that can achieve strategic objectives and choices;
- an analysis aimed at quantifying the strategic design on economic, financial and capital levels;
- an analysis aimed at preparing a formal strategic plan.

THE ACTION PLAN: AN ANALYSIS
OF POSSIBLE INTERVENTIONS

An action plan is that part of an overall strategy project that identifies the most important projects, or courses of action, necessary to carry out strategic choices and achieve competitive goals. An action plan is actually a list of things to do that clearly specifies timeframes and interim deadlines, persons in charge and responsibilities, costs and investments required to complete the plan.

The questions that an analysis should normally answer concerning the action plan are mainly the following.

- Given the current resources, capabilities and competences, as well as the competitive objectives and strategic choices, which planned activities should be undertaken to carry out the project?
- What impact will the planned actions have on resources, capabilities and competences? What will be the impact on firm organization?
- Are the planned actions feasible? With what tactics? How will they fit in with normal business activities?

An action plan can involve any aspect of firm life: reduction of staff, expansion of the sales network, renegotiation of distribution agreements, a merger with a competitor and so on. Its extension and outline depend on many variables. First, we must consider the degree of discontinuity that the new competitive objectives and strategy choices would bring about in the organization. In principle, if the objectives and choices are conservative, then the impact on company organization should be modest and the action plan not particularly complex or too detailed. On the other hand, if the strategic choices include a vast reconfiguration of competitive processes and necessary resources, then the action plan will prove to be quite challenging. Its complexity also depends on the type of organization and particularly on how familiar the organization is with project management. Basically, an action plan identifies a number of projects to be completed within a specified period.

Because an action plan focuses on the achievement of strategy projects, and therefore includes only those activities that are directly aimed at achieving competitive objectives and strategic choices, a crucial aspect is to find a balance between plans aimed at the implementation of strategic choices and normal business operations. An action plan can have a more or less profound impact on these activities, but their continuity must be guaranteed.

A substantial part of the success or failure of a strategic design is played out on this shaky ground of balance between strategic innovation, more or less extensive, and organizational routine. Is the strategic plan sustainable?

The analyst's task in preparing an action plan may be briefly described by the following steps:

1. to identify potential projects instrumental to carrying out strategic choices;
2. to define an order of priority for the various potential projects planned;
3. to provide an initial outline of the projects (deadlines, responsibilities, resources, important decisions, etc.);
4. to make sure that the various projects are coherent with each other and that there is overall compatibility between competitive objectives, strategic decisions and the potential projects planned;
5. to facilitate the final choice of which projects to include in the action plan.

COMPETITIVE STRUCTURE AND ECONOMIC EVALUATION

After drawing up an action plan, the analysis continues by focusing on what would happen to the firm's economic, financial and capital situation once the strategic design has been completed. In this case, the questions that drive the analytical process are obvious.

What will happen to the firm's capital situation should the strategic design be achieved? How will the capacity to generate income change? And how will it change financial stability?

Is the strategic plan sustainable? Which and how many risks are involved?

How much is the business actually worth in light of the strategy design?

Strategic decisions and an action plan will change the competitive structure and consequently the 'trajectory' that the financial situation would have taken without the planned intervention. When thinking about the economic and financial impacts of strategic decisions and an action plan, it may be helpful to introduce the concept of strategic differential.

In every moment of its life, a company has a given capital structure, which for our purposes can be represented by a functional reclassification of assets, which essentially consists in grouping assets and liabilities in relation to the nature of management operations (Figure 7.1).

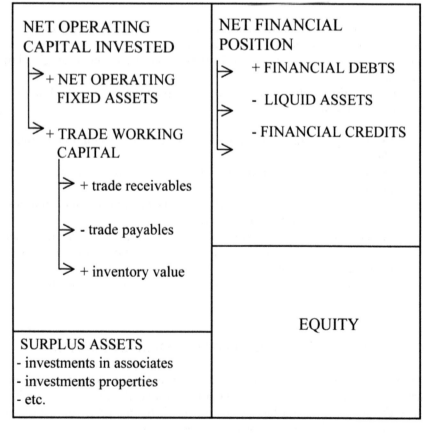

Figure 7.1 Functional reclassification of assets.

Invested capital is essentially net operating capital invested, which in turn consists of the net operating fixed assets (tangibles, intangibles and financial assets) and working capital (trade receivables less trade debts plus inventory value). This capital is intended for operational purposes and differs from any ancillary activities, (surplus assets) namely from those uses that would not have any direct impact on operations; normally included among these are investments in associates (except in the case that they take on an operational role) or investments properties. Concerning capital sources, however, the significant distinction is between the net financial position, or net debt (debt net of cash and financial assets) and equity.

Now the competitive structure corresponds to a given capital structure, according to the following representation of:

$$A_0 = I_0 = D_0 + E_0$$

where
A_0 = competitive structure at time t_0
I_0 = capital invested at time t_0
D_0 = net debt at time t_0
E_0 = equity at time t_0

The competitive structure will change over time even without any planned intervention. Let's suppose that a three-year strategic plan will have changed by the end of that period both the competitive structure and the capital structure as follows:

$$A_3 = I_3 = D_3 + E_3$$

We define strategic differential as the difference between the initial competitive structure and the final competitive structure, measured by the change in capital structure. Thus, the strategic differential D will be:

$$D = I_3 - I_0 = (D_3 - D_0) + (E_3 - E_0)$$

The differential can be expressed in several ways. In particular, we can calculate the percentage of change in money spent and the percentage of change in the mix between debt and equity. More precisely:

- changes in capital invested in the period = $\Delta I_n = \dfrac{I_n - I_0}{I_0}$

- changes in equity during the period = $\Delta E_n = \dfrac{E_n - E_0}{E_0}$

- changes in debt during the period = $\Delta D_n = \dfrac{D_n - D_0}{D_0}$

- weighting of equity = $PE = \dfrac{E_0}{E_0 + D_0}$

- weighting of debt capital = $PD = \dfrac{D_0}{E_0 + D_0}$

You can use the resulting formula to quantitatively assess the strategic differential:

$$D = \Delta I = \Delta D \times PD + \Delta E \times PE$$

Any strategic design can be interpreted in advance in terms of the strategic differential, namely in terms of asset changes that will result if the plan is fully implemented within the established time period. In other words, a strategic design can be evaluated in terms of asset changes that will have effectively taken place by the end of the established period. Of course, that is not the only way to evaluate the success of a plan, and not necessarily the right way. For example, a plan may have obtained the predetermined differential but through competition that is inconsistent with the strategic choices. In quantitative terms, however, it may be helpful to:

- define *ex ante* the implicit differential in the strategic design;
- verify during the on-going project whether you are gradually attaining the desired conditions of the differential;
- determine *ex post* whether the desired differential is consistent with the differential obtained.

THE STRATEGIC DESIGN'S ECONOMIC, CAPITAL AND FINANCIAL PROSPECTS

In order to quantify any changes in assets, you must have access to economic forecasting, *pro forma* balance sheets and expected cash flows—all projected along the design's timeframe.

Figures 7.2, 7.3 and 7.4 illustrate standard forms for income statements, financial statements and cash flow statements, respectively. Below are some observations, not on individual items, but on the structure of the charts.

The prospects are subject to various forms, beginning with the timescale that has to coincide with the timeframe assigned to the strategic design. The time periods normally used range from three to five years. In principle, the timeframe should coincide with the number of years necessary to achieve the competitive objectives set out in the design.

Another fundamental aspect concerns the different positionings a firm has assumed on the market. If the company meets several needs, and therefore has several strategic positionings, then the forecasts need to be verified, at least those concerning the economic situation and, if possible, the assets situation must be checked for each individual positioning.

Note that the situation for each positioning may coincide with the most well-known situation for the business's strategic area, with more organizational worth per strategic business unit. It is almost impossible and essentially useless to evaluate a given positioning based on cash flow, unless in highly segmented fields. In fact, you are more likely to encounter difficulties

	2012	Δ%	2013	Δ%	2014	Δ%
1. NET REVENUES (%)						
2. Cost of goods sold (%)						
3. = GROSS MARGIN (%)						
4. Fixed cots (%)						
5. = (%) (EBITDA)						
6. Amortizations and depreciations						
7. = (%) EBIT						
8. Interest expenses (%)						
9. +/- one-offs cost/income (%)						
10. = INCOME BEFORE TAXES (%)						
11. Tax expenses (%)						
12. = NET INCOME (%)						

Figure 7.2 Income statement.

	2012	Δ%	2013	Δ%	2014	Δ%
1. Trade receivables						
2. Inventory						
3. Trade payables						
4. TRADE WORKING CAPITAL (1 + 2 - 3)						
5. Net tangible assets						
6. Net intangible assets						
7. Financial assets						
8. NET FIXED ASSETS (5 + 6 + 7)						
9. Employee benefits						
10. OPERATING NET INVESTED CAPITAL (4 + 8 - 9)						
11. Surplus assets						
12 NET INVESTED CAPITAL (10 + 11)						
13 Financial debts						
14. Financial credits						
15. Liquid assets						
16. NET FINANCIAL POSITION (13 - 14 - 15)						
17. Tax provision						
18. Equity						
19. TOTAL COVERAGE (16 + 17 + 18)						

Figure 7.3   Financial statement.

	2012	2013	2014
1. Gross margin			
2. ± Trade working capital variation			
3. ± Variation in employee benefit			
4. - Acquisition of operating investments			
5. + Disinvestments of assets			
6. = OPERATING CASH FLOW			
7. ± Net surplus assets cash flow			
7. ± Interests (paid / received)			
9. - Dividends paid			
10. ± Variation in stock capital			
11. - Taxes			
12. ± Variation in tax provisions			
13. = NET FINANCIAL POSITION FLOW			
Broken down in:			
* Debts repayment			
* New financings			
* Liquid assets decrease			
* Liquid assets increase			

Figure 7.4   Cash flow statement.

in assessing the financial situation, especially the balance sheet; everything will depend on the effectiveness of the information system used by the firm.

The level of positioning assessment should be pushed up to a point considered reasonable and economically significant and which could reach the EBITDA positioning or operating income positioning for the income statement (Figure 7.5) and working capital or net invested capital (which does not usually include financial assets) at the financial statement level (Figure 7.6).

For example, the possibility and opportunity to allocate a share of employee benefit to positioning will depend on the possibility of regularly allocating part of the staff to one positioning rather than another.

Appropriate summary and reconciliation tables will allow us to visualize the role and contribution of each positioning when preparing a strategic design (Figures 7.7 and 7.8).

Finally, some further considerations of a more technical nature.

Nothing prevents one from addressing other aspects which may be even more analytical (actually, in some cases it might even be helpful or essential). Reference is often made to a firm's specific structure, for instance by

1. = POSITIONING NET REVENUES (%)
4. – Variable cost of goods sold (%)
5. = POSITIONING GROSS MARGIN (%)
6. – Positioning fixed costs (%)
7. = POSITIONING EBITDA (%)
8. – Positioning amortizations and depreciations (%)
9. = POSITIONING EBIT

Figure 7.5 Positioning income statement.

1. Positioning trade receivables
2. Positioning inventory
3. Positioning trade payables
4. POSITIONING TRADE WORKING CAPITAL (1 + 2 - 3)
5. Positioning net tangible assets
6. Positioning net intangible assets
7. POSITIONING NET FIXED CAPITAL (5 + 6)
8. Positioning employees benefits
9. POSITIONING NET OPERATING CAPITAL INVESTED (4 + 7 + 8)

Figure 7.6 Positioning financial statement.

product/service, brand, region, distribution channels, etc. But in any case, because the level of diversification does not determine management control (which always requires an important in-depth analysis) but concerns the overall assessment of a strategic design's economic, financial and capital implications, this level must serve to reconstruct the absorption process and generate worth, and will be assessed on a case by case basis.

In the event that the strategic design provides for expansion through acquisitions, and that such acquisitions are not yet certain at the time of plan development, it is also a good idea to come up with a strategic scenario that does not include any acquisitions. The same holds true when any sales or transfers, mergers or entry of new uncertain capital is foreseen.

In the event that the strategic design involves a group, certain rules should be followed regarding economic, financial and capital implications.

	Pos. 1	Pos. N	Overall firm
1. Positioning gross revenues			
2. - Deductions			
3. = POSITIONING NET REVENUES (%)			
4. - Positioning variable cost of goods sold (%)			
5. = POSITIONING GROSS MARGIN (%)			
6. - Positioning fixed costs (%)			
7. = POSITIONING EBIT (%)			
8. – Positioning amortization(%)			
9. = POSITIONING EBITDA (%)			
10. ± Revenues and variable cost of goods sold not attributable to positioning			
11. = GROSS MARGIN (%) (5 + 10)			
12. – Fixed costs not attributable to positioning (%)			
13. = EBIT(%) (7 - 12)			
14. – Amortization not attributable to positioning (%)			
15. = EBITDA (%) (9 - 14)			
16. – Interests expenses (%)			
17. ± Exceptional items (%)			
18. = INCOME BEFORE TAX (%)			
19. – Tax expenses (%)			
20. = NET INCOME (%)			

Figure 7.7 Role and contribution of each positioning.

Broadly speaking, the group (intended in an industrial sense) should be treated as a single entity. The fact that a group comprises various companies and that there may be minor interests does not alter the basic structure of economic implications, for both the group at large and individual positionings. You should definitely consider the significance of intercompany transactions very carefully and, in principle, exclude them from the individual positionings' income statements (if an individual positioning corresponds to a certain company).

How are economic situations 'moved'? In what way are they projected along the reference period? There is no single technique or, more generally, a single way. The following logic based on several steps has been proposed.

First, after having reclassified and standardized the latest available summary data, you need to know what the firm's key value drivers (KVD) are, meaning the main determinants of the profitability, capital and financial profiles. The KVDs change considerably depending on the nature of a firm's activities, namely in relation to the type of technology used to prepare the supply. The literature contains actual models of analysis required to identify the various KVDs (Copeland, Koller and Murrin 1990). In different ways, an attempt has been made to link the mathematical relationships between operating income, net capital and net cash flow from operations (output

	Pos. 1	Pos. N	Overall firm
1. Positioning trade receivables			
2. Positioning inventory			
3. Positioning trade payables			
4. POSITIONING WORKING TRADE CAPITAL (1 + 2 - 3)			
5. Positioning net tangible assets			
6. Positioning net intangible assets			
7. POSITIONING FIXED CAPITAL (5 +6)			
8. Positioning employee benefits			
9. POSITIONING NET OPERATING CAPITAL INVESTED (4 + 7 + 8)			
10. Working trade capital not attributable to positioning			
11. Fixed capital not attributable to positioning			
12. Employees benefits not attributable to positioning			
13. NET OPERATING CAPITAL INVESTED (9 + 10 + 11 -12)			
14. Surplus assets			
15. INVESTED CAPITAL (13 + 14)			
16. Financial debts			
17. Financial credits			
18. Liquid assets			
19. NET FINANCIAL POSITION (16 - 17 - 18)			
20. Tax provision			
21. Equity			
22. TOTAL COVERAGE (19 + 20 + 21)			

Figure 7.8   Role and contribution of each positioning (bis).

variables) with certain input variables, or determinants, which relate to the main directional levers.

Once the key value drivers have been identified on the basis of historical results, you can use them to predict economic and financial situations in the future. Naturally, at this point both the competitive objectives and assumptions on which the strategic design was developed come into play. Everything considered, we can then envisage what the economic, financial and capital trends might be over the time period considered.

The process will vary rather significantly depending on what sort of technology the company uses. We can make a rough distinction between firms that produce in series, those that operate on vast distribution scales and those that work on job orders. For companies that produce in series, the essential inventory forecast concerns market trends and the company's market share (in this sense we speak of a 'top down' type approach that starts from expected market trends in general and ends with the individual company and its market share). From a resource absorption point of view, the use of standard costs is of great importance to these companies.

For companies operating in mass distribution, however, the approach is a 'bottom up' type, where the starting point is not with market trends but with the sales volumes for the various stores that sell different product categories. Of course, scenario variables, ranging, for example, from the economic situation to the inflation rate and the social behavior of consumers, assume considerable significance when moving from historic results to forecasts for the reference time period.

Finally, regarding businesses operating on order, we start from orders received and the forecasts for their completion (times that will consequentially depend on how the key economic, capital and financial situations change as time goes by). Another fundamental factor of forecasting is the order book, its recent trends and the assumptions relating to its future development. To arrive at such predictions, you need specific information such as the investment plans of customers who place orders with your company (which can be public or private) and past success rates (percentage of tenders won out of total participation).

STRATEGIC DESIGN AND VALUE

The connection between a strategic design and enterprise value is very strong and should be carefully considered in any planning phase.

A strategic design, whose specific objectives will have an effect on how the competitive structure will change, is actually a plan to create value. We can say that a strategic design set up at time t_0 is linked to a certain reference deadline t_n and it will have a given strategic differential, at least in intention, and at the same time will involve some assessment of the firm at time t_0.

How much is the enterprise value driven by a strategic design?

The economic, financial and capital implications of the strategic design and its impact on possible risk conditions allow us to associate the following formula for enterprise value with the plan, taken as a set of activities:

$$VA_0 = \sum_{t=1}^{T} \frac{FCFO_t}{[1+ke(U)]^t} + \sum_{t=1}^{T} \frac{D_T \times kd \times tc}{(1+kd)^T} + \frac{TV_{unlelered}}{[1+ke(U)]^T} + \frac{TV_{TS}}{(1+kd)^T}$$

$VA_0 =$	value of company assets at time t_0
$FCFO_t =$	net operating cash flows in year t
$ke\,(U) =$	cost of equity capital in the absence of debt
$D_T =$	debt at the end of plan period T
$kd =$	cost of debt
$tc =$	tax rate applied to taxable income
$TV_{unlevered} =$	unlevered terminal value calculated at the end of plan period T
$TV_{TS} =$	terminal value of tax benefits for debt calculated at the end of plan period T

For every strategic design it is therefore possible to associate some measure of value, whether the value of economic capital (equity value), the value of all assets (enterprise value) or the value of goodwill. Based on these relationships, the analyst can develop some helpful insights concerning *ex ante* decisions and the *ex post* control process of implementing the strategic design.

For example, the total value of corporate assets calculated at the beginning of the plan with reference to the end of the period will be found by the change in value of posted assets (strategic differential) and by a value of goodwill at time t_n.

$$VA_0 = A_0 + (A_n - A_0) + G$$

It is therefore possible to come up with a summary assessment of the changes that the strategic plan will bring about concerning the value established for all assets (strategic differential) and the degree of goodwill by identifying four typical situations (Figure 7.9).

1. A strategic design that involves low strategic differential and goodwill can be defined, in terms of value, as being conservative.
2. However, when the strategic differential is high and goodwill low, then the strategic plan will involve expansion based on an increase in invested capital (usually tangible).
3. Whenever a strategic design brings with it high goodwill and low strategic differential, we can generally claim that it is based on the

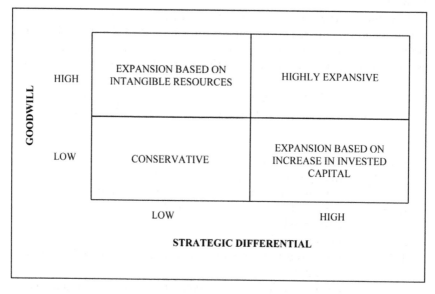

Figure 7.9   Strategic differential and goodwill.

development of intangible resources, namely organizational conditions that will not find a corresponding book value (or which are not, at any rate, individually assessed assets).

4. Finally, when both goodwill and the strategic differential are high, we are faced with a highly expansive strategic design which drives both value dimensions.

Another way to reason on the implications that a strategic design will have, regarding enterprise value, is to use information on the changes in economic variables in terms of competitive positioning, rather than overall positioning. The breakdown is particularly significant if you are working along two dimensions of analysis:

1. working capital invested in specific competitive positioning;
2. the spread expected between ROI and WACC concerning a single positioning.

Again, you will find four typical situations where you can place each positioning chosen by the firm (Figure 7.10).

Positioning from which the company expects a lower return on invested capital than the cost of capital and which requires an investment of working capital below the average level (if overall investment in working capital in the business is 100, for example, the average value is equal to 50). These

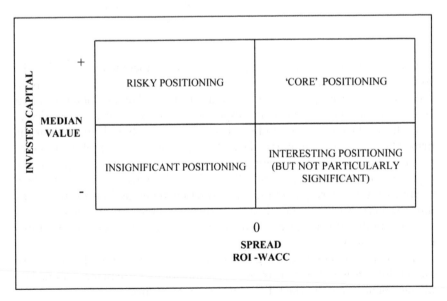

Figure 7.10   Positioning assessment: invested capital and spread.

are seemingly insignificant positionings which can, however, be a good choice in a broader competitive framework.

When the invested capital remains low but the expected returns are higher than the cost of capital, we are faced with an interesting positioning, even though, given the low value of the investment, it will not bring a particularly significant overall return in absolute value.

The opposite situation has high capital investments and modest expected profits. In this case, which is risky, there must be some very good reasons to maintain this positioning in the strategic design.

The last case of positioning is where high profitability is associated with consistent operating investments. These are the company's 'core' positionings.

THE STRATEGIC PLAN

Once completed, the strategic design should be formalized and written up in a document that is called the strategic plan.

The questions that typically guide this final phase of the analysis process are usually the following:

- What are the objectives to be pursued in setting up a business plan? Who are the key internal and, if any, external players?
- What is the plan format (content and illustration mode) that is considered most appropriate, given the objectives of the business plan and the nature and characteristics of the strategy plan? Is it necessary to prepare the plan in several formats for different uses? What would these be?

On a strictly logical level, the preparation of a document containing the strategic plan is not absolutely necessary for the existence of the overall project. However, the preparation of an overall strategic plan, or a document that clearly outlines the strategic plan, responds to several important objectives.

It allows the entire plan and single choices to be shared throughout the firm. The action plan, in particular, allows the enterprise to relate the competitive objectives and strategic choices to those aims that weigh on the organizational structure, potentially at all levels. This way the entire firm organization takes responsibility with obvious repercussions on the continuity and effectiveness of evaluation systems and incentive schemes.

It facilitates the project's control process and implementation status (strategic control).

It clarifies the competitive goals that the company intends to achieve and in this sense makes it clear which responsibilities are being assumed by management, typically the CEO and the board of directors.

It makes communication possible even outside of the strategic plan, with information limitations that are cleared up as the case arises.

Communication outside the strategic plan is probably the most interesting feature of recent years. The need to clearly express the competitive objectives, strategic choices and any economic and financial impacts, which will not only affect the organization but the stakeholders as well (financial analysts, customers, banks, suppliers, etc.), is a consequence of the gradual intensification of the systemic nature of a company and the more intense competition in the acquisition of critical resources.

However, the amount of information that is given to external parties is generally not the same for different stakeholders. In other words, different targets require different levels of detail and different modes of communication. In this sense, in terms of communication, the plan may take a flexible and modular form that will be adapted from time to time to the current need. This way, too, the difference between a strategic plan, which is always a single, integrated project, and a strategic design, which is the document that presents it, is clearly evident and as such may take various forms, depending on the objectives of communication.

Concerning these last considerations, defining a standard format for a business plan is likely to be a feckless exercise.

However, there are some things that generally need to be expressed that will be helpful within the firm, typically for managerial purposes. In fact, if these are the goals, we could say very simply that there is only one rule: The strategic plan must contain the entire strategic design. Thus it must always clearly state the four key components of the strategic plan: competitive objectives, strategic choices, action plan and economic and financial implications. Different is the case of the analytical material used to support those decisions, which may appear in the business plan in more or less detail. Think on the assumptions or key value drivers: both of these are not necessarily formalized in business plans (and here again the nature of the stakeholder to whom the plan is presented becomes significant and, thus, the modulation of the plan itself). Ultimately, if you want to create a general reference model, the following typical structure can be used for a strategic plan:

- description of the current competitive structure, enriched by the company's mission, that would allow one to recognize the company's reference values;
- competitive and economic results achieved in each historically addressed positioning, combined with information about profitability;
- needs/opportunities for growth of or changes in the competitive structure;
- brief description of the strategic vision, or of the main competitive objectives and value to be achieved during the plan period;

- main hypotheses or assumptions relating to the competitive, general and industrial scenarios (and possible illustration of analyses conducted);
- choices of positioning and choices relating to the technology portfolio;
- competitive objectives for each chosen positioning (target size, positioning, key factors);
- configuration of the competitive process and other solutions that the company intends to adopt in relation to the acquisition and use of resources;
- action plan, with an outline of main activities;
- main hypotheses regarding key value drivers (and possible illustration of analyses conducted);
- economic and financial implications, with the possible publication of the sensitivity analysis developed.

CONCLUSIONS: PROJECT IMPLEMENTATION AND CONTINUOUS PLANNING

It would be unwise to make a net distinction between the strategic planning phase and the implementation phase; in reality, planning and implementation, in many ways, proceed, or should proceed, along parallel tracks. You must be aware, however, that introducing a strategic project into current management is always a highly crucial time, with the risk of misalignment between the strategic choices and usual decision-making and behavioral habits of the different actors involved.

Transforming a strategic design into a strategic plan, meaning the formal document specifically drawn up to express and explain the strategy, is the first step that will essentially help the organization 'metabolize' the strategic choices. The action plan and the economic and financial implications, in particular, must become benchmarks from which all the main operating mechanisms, from budgeting to the reward system, will be consistently modeled.

The project (and thus the plan), including the long-term focus that normally characterizes it, must be a permanently ongoing 'workshop' that is subject to change, even substantial change, in response to changes that may emerge over time with regard to the competitive environment, decisions made and business requirements. In this sense, a strategic project is a continuous process, driven by analysis, as has already been said, and strategic control, which has two main purposes:

- to continuously and systematically verify the sustainability of competitive objectives and the effectiveness of strategic choices;
- to continuously and systematically verify to what extent the competitive goals have been achieved, the strategic choices have been

carried out and finally, how many of the planned activities have been implemented.

Figure 7.11 provides an example of the entire process in a timeline, indicating the beginning and end of each step (evaluation of the competitive structure, preparation of the strategic plan and formal written preparation of the business plan). In the example, the strategic plan and strategic design are redefined each year, moving the reference timeline up one year (in our case we went from the project or plan 2011–2013 to the project/plan 2012–2014). The strategic analysis, strategic control and implementation of the plan are continuous activities, although the analysis requires a more intense period that runs from the evaluation of the competitive structure to the final definition of the strategic plan.

Note that the relationship between the two plans (2011–2013 and 2012–2014) can be of different kinds, depending on the case. At the extremes:

- the projects can be substantially the same, the only difference being the shift in timing;
- the projects can be radically different.

Whether we tend toward the first or second case depends on many factors, including the degree of implementation of the current plan, the emergence of new opportunities and new risks, relationships with investors and so on. However, the results of the analysis and strategic control will suggest either a conservative (keeping the basic structure of the plan) or a revolutionary approach (radical change in the structure).

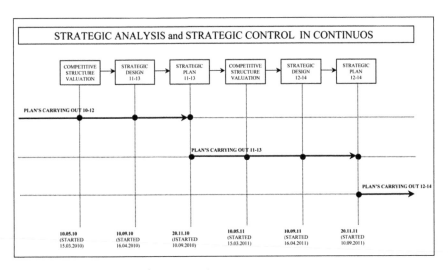

Figure 7.11   Strategic analysis in continuous.

Bibliography

Abell, D. F. (1980) *Defining the Business: The Strategy Point of Strategic Planning*, Prentice Hall, Englewood Cliffs, New Jersey.

Ambrosini, V., C. Bowman, and N. Collier (2009) "Dynamic Capabilities: An Exploration of How Firms Renew Their Resource Base", *British Journal of Management*, 20: S9–S24.

Ambrosini, V., G. Johnson, and K. Scholes (1998) *Exploring Techniques of Analysis and Evaluation in Strategic Management*, McGraw-Hill, New York.

Amit, R., and P. J. H. Schoemaker (1993) "Strategic Assets and Organizational Rent", *Strategic Management Journal*, 14: 33–46.

Andrews, K. R. (1964) *A Concept of Corporate Strategy*, presented at the 11th meeting of Institute of Management Science, Pittsburgh, April 14, 1964.

———. (1971) *Corporate Strategy*, McGraw-Hill, New York.

Ansoff, H. I. (1965) *Corporate Strategy*, McGraw-Hill, New York.

———. (1968) *Corporate Strategy: An Analytic Approach to Business Policy for Growth and Expansion*, McGraw-Hill, New York.

———. (1987) "The Emerging Paradigm of Strategic Behavior", *Strategic Management Journal*, 8: 501–515.

Baaij, M., M. Greeven, and J. Van Dalen (2004) "Persistent Superior Economic Performance, Sustainable Competitive Advantage, and Schumpeterian Innovation: Leading Established Computer Firms, 1954–2000", *European Management Journal*, 22(5): 517–531.

Bain, J.S. (1951) "Relation of Profit Rate to Industry Concentration: American Manufacturing, 1936-1940", *Quarterly Journal of Economics*, 3: 293-324.

Barney, J. B. (1986) "Strategic Factor Markets: Expectations, Luck, and Business Strategy", *Management Science*, 32(10): 1231–1241.

———. (1991) "Firm resources and sustained competitive advantage", *Journal of Management*, 17: 99–120.

Barney, J. B., and R. W. Griffin (1992) *The Management of Organisation: Strategy, Structure, Behaviour*, Houghton Mifflin Company, Boston, Massachusetts.

Barney, J. B., and R. E. Hoskisson (1990) "Strategic Groups: Untestsed Assertions and Research Proposal", *Managerial and Decision Economics*, 11: 187–198.

Baumol, W.J. and Panzer, J.C. and Willig, R.D. (1982) *Contestable Markets and the Theory of Industry Structure*, Harcourt, New York.

Beretta Zanoni, A. (1997) *Strategia e Politica Aziendale negli Studi Italiani e Internazionali*, Giuffrè Editore, Milano.

———. (2008) *Strategia Aziendale: Teoria e Processi Decisionali*, Cedam, Padova.

———. (2009) *Il Governo Strategico dell'Impresa*, Egea, Milano.

Beretta Zanoni, A., and S. Colombo (2010) "I value drivers della distintività", *concept paper of Business Strategy research group*, January 2010, No.2, available on-line at www.gdrstrategia.com, date access, October 2010.

Besanko, D., D. Dranove, and S. Shanley (2006) *Economics of Strategy*, John Wiley & Sons, Hoboken, New Jersey.

Bontis, N. (1996) "There is a Proce on Your Head: Managing Intellectual Capital Strategically", *Ivey Business Journal* (formerly *Business Quarterly*), Summer: 40–47.

Bower, G. L. (1970) *Managing the Resource Allocation Process*, Irwin Inc., Homewood, Illinois.

Bower, J. L., and C. M. Christensen (1995) "Disruptive Technologies: Catching the Wave", *Harvard Business Review*, January–February, reprint 95103, 43–53.

Bresser-Pereira, L. C. (2009) "The two methods and the hard core of economics", *Revista de Economia Política*, 29(2).

Brock, D. M. (2006) "The Changing Professional Organization: A Review of Competing Archetypes", *International Journal of Management Reviews*, 8(3):157–174.

Brooking, A. (1996) *Intellectual Capital: Core Assets for the Third Millennium Enterprise*, Thomson Business Press, London, United Kingdom.

Bryman, A., and E. Bell (2007) *Business Research Methods*, Oxford University Press, Oxford.

Buzzell, R. D., and B. T. Gale (1987) *The PIMS Principles*, Free Press, New York.

Cabral, L. (2002) *Economia Industriale*, Carocci Editore.

Chan Kim, W., and R. Mauborgne (2005) *Blue Ocean Strategy: How to Create Unconstested Market Space and Make Competition Irrelevant*, Harvard Business School Press, Boston, Massachusetts.

Chandler, A. (1963) *Strategy and Stucture*, Prentice Hall, New Jersey.

Changanti, R., and R. Sambrharya (1987) "Strategic Orientation and Characteristics of Upper Management", *Strategic Management Journal*, 8(4): 393–401.

Christensen, C. M. (1997) *The Innovator's Dilemma*, Harvard Business School Press, Boston, Massachusetts.

Cockburn, I. M., R. M. Henderson, and S. Stern (2000) "Untangling the Origins of Competitive Advantage", *Strategic Management Journal*, 21: 1123–1145.

Coda, V. (1988) *L'Orientamento Strategico di Impresa*, Utet, Torino.

Collins, D.J. and Montgomery C.A. (1997) *Corporate Strategy*, McGraw-Hill, Chicago.

Copeland, T., T. Koller, and J. Murrin (1990) *Valuation: Measuring and Managing the Value of Companies*, Wiley Finance, McKinsey and Co. Inc.

Coyle, G. (2004) *Practical Strategy: Structured Tools and Techniques*, Prentice Hall, New Jersey.

D'Aveni, R. A., G. B. Dagnino, and K. B. Smith (2010) "Special Issue: The Age of Temporary Advantages", *Strategic Management Journal*, 21(13): 1371–1389.

Dierickx, I., and K. Cool (1989) "Assets Stock Accumulation and Sustainability of Competitive Advantage", *Management Science*, 35(12): 1504–1511.

Edvinsson, L., and M. S. Malone (1997) *Intellectual Capital: Realizing Your Company's True Value by Finding Its Hidden Brainpower*, Harper Business, New York.

Faulkner, D., and C. Bowman (1995) *The Essence of Competitive Strategy*, Prentice Hall, New York.

Fischer, F. (1991) *Industrial Organization, Economics, and the Law*, Cambridge, MIT Press, Boston, Massachusetts.

Franco, R., M.B Sarkar, R. Argwal and R. Echambedi. (2009) "Moderating Effects of Technological Capabilities on Market Pioneering-Firm Survival Relationship", *Management Science*, 55(11).

Galan, J. I., and M. J. Sanchez-Bueno (2009) "Strategy and Structure in context: Universalism versus institutional effects", 30(6): 609–627.

Galbraith, C., and D. Schendel (1983) "An Empirical Analysis of Strategy Types", *Strategic Management Journal*, 4(2): 153–173.

Ghemawat, P. (1997) *Games Businesses Play: Cases and Models*, MIT Press, Boston, Massachusetts.

Gibbons, R. (1996) *A Primer in Game Theory*, Financial Times, Prentice Hall, New York.

Grant, R. (1988) *Contemporary Strategy Analysis*, Blackwell, Malden, Massachusetts.

Greenwood, R., and C. R. Hinings (1993) "Understanding Strategic Change: The Contribution of Archetypes", *Academy of Management Journal*, 36(5): 1052–1081.

Hamel, G. (1998) "Strategy Innovation and the Quest for Value", *Sloan Management Review*, Winter: 7–14.

Hamel, G. (2000) *Leading the Revolution*, Harvard Business School Press, Boston, Massachusetts.

Hamel, G., and C. K. Prahalad (1990) "The Core Competences of the Corporation", *Harvard Business Review*, 68(3): 537–556.

———. (1993) "Strategy as Stretch and Leverage", *Harvard Business Review*, 75–84.

Hax, A., and N. Majluf (1996) *The Strategy Concept and Process: A Pragmatic Approach*, 2nd edition, Prentice Hall, New Jersey.

Hitt, M. A., R. D. Ireland, and R. E. Hoskisson (2005) *Strategic Management: Competitiveness and Globalization*, 6th edition, South-Western, Versailles, Kentucky.

Hofer, C. H., and D. Schendel (1978) *Strategy Formulation: Analytical Concepts*, West Pub. Co. Eagan, MN.

Hoopes, D. G., T. L. Madsen, and G. Walker (2003) "Special Issue: Why Is There a Resource-Based View? Toward a Theory of Competitive Heterogeneity", *Strategic Management Journal*, 24(10): 889–902.

Johnson, G., and K. Scholes (2002) *Exploring Corporate Strategy: Text and Cases*, Prentice Hall, London.

Jovanivic, B. (1982) "Selection and the Evolution of Industry.", *Econometrica*, 50: 649-70.

Kaplan, R. S., and D. P. Norton (1992) "The Balanced Scorecard Measures that Drive Performance", *Harvard Business Review*, January–February, 71–79.

Kay, J. (1993) *"A Brief History of Business Strategy"*, in J. Kay (ed.), *The Economics of Business Strategy. The International Library of Critical Writings in Economics 163*, Edward Elgar Publishing Limited, Glensada House, United Kingdom.

Ketchen, D. J., and C. L. Shook (1996) "The Application of Cluster Analysis in Strategic Management Research: An Analysis and Critique", *Strategic Management Journal*, 17(6): 441–458.

Klepper, S. (1997) "Industry Life Cycle", *Industrial and Corporate Change* 6(1): 145-182.

Kotler, P. (1972) *Marketing Management*, Prentice-Hall, Englewood Cliffs, NJ.

Lee, A. S., and G. S. Hubona (2009) "A Scientific Basis for Rigor in Information Systems Research", *MIS Quarterly*, 33(2): 237–262.

Lev, B. (1999) "R&D and Capital Markets", *Journal of Applied Corporate Finance*, 11(4): 21–35.

———. (2002) "Rethinking Accounting", *Financial Executive*, April–March, 34–39.

Levitt, T. (1965) "Exploit the Product Life Cycle", *Harvard Business Review*, 43, November–December: 81–94.

Lieberman, M. B. (1987) "Strategies for Capacity Expansion", *Sloan Management Review*, Summer 1987: 19–25.

Malerba, F. and L Orsenigo (1996), "The Dynamics and Evolution of Industries", *Industrial and Corporate Change*, 5, 51-87.

Maksimovick, V. and Phillips G. and Prabhala N.R. (2008), "Post-Merger Restructuring and the Boundaries of the Firm", NBER Working Paper, No. 14291.

Mansifield, G. M., and L. C. H. Fourie (2004) "Strategy and Business Models—Strange Bedfellows? A Case for Convergence and its Evolution into Strategic Architecture", *South African Journal of Business Managenent*, 35(1): 35–44.

McGahan, A. M., and M. Porter (1997) "How much does Strategy matter, really?", *Strategic Management Journal*, 18(1): 15–30.

McNamara, G., D. L. Deephouse, and R. A. Luce (2003) "Competitive Positioning within and across a Strategic Group Structure: The Performance of Core, Secondary and Solitary Firms", *Strategic Management Journal*, 24(2): 161–181.

McPherson, J. (1998) "Inclusive Valuation Methodology", cited in Skyrme (1999), Measuring the Value of Knowledge. Business Intelligence.

Miles, R. E., and C. C. Snow (1978) *Organizational Strategy, Structure and Process*, McGraw-Hill, New York.

Narayanan, V. K., and L. Fahey (2001) "Macroenvironmental Analysis: Understanding the Environment Outside the Industry", in L. Fahey & R. M. Randall (eds.), *The Portable MBA in Strategy*, 2nd edition, John Wiley & Sons Inc., New York.

Newbert, S. L. (2008) "Value, Rareness, Competitive Advantage, and Performance: A Conceptual-Level Empirical Investigation of the Resources Based View of the Firm", *Strategic Management Journal*, 29(7): 745–768.

Normann, R. (1977) *Management for Growth*, John Wiley and Sons, Chichester.

O'Shaughnessy, J. (1995) *Competitive Marketing: A Strategic Approach*, Routledge, London and New York.

Pattison, D.D., Teplitz, C.J (1989) "Are Learning Curves still Relevant?", *Management Accounting*, 70(8): 37-40.

Penrose, E. (1959) *The Theory of Growth of Firm*, Oxford University Press, New York.

Peteraf, M. A. (1993) "The Cornerstones of Competitive Advantage: A Resource-Based View", *Strategic Management Journal*, No.14, 170–181.

Porter, M. (1980) *Competitive Strategy*, The Free Press, NewYork.

———. (1985) *Competitive Advantage*, The Free Press, New York.

Robinson, R. B., and J. A. Pearce (1988) "Planned Patterns of Strategic Behavior and Their Relationship to Business-Unit Performance", *Strategic Management Journal*, 9(1): 43–60.

Roquebert, J. A., R. L. Phillips, and P. A. Westfall (1996) "Market vs Management: What 'Drives' Profitabilty?", *Strategic Management Journal*, 17(8): 653–664.

Rumelt, R. (1984) 'Towards a Strategic Theory of the Firm', in R. B. Lamb (ed.), *Competitive Strategic Management*, 556–570, Prentice Hall, Englewood Cliffs, New Jersey.

———. (1991) "How Much Does Industry Matter?", *Strategic Management Journal*, Vol 12: 167–185.

Sanchez, R. (2001) *"Managing knowledge into compentences: The five learning cycles of competent organization"*, 3–37, in *Knowledge Management and Organizational Competences*, R. Sanchez (ed.), Oxford University Press, Oxford.

Schmalensee, R. (1985) "Do Markets Differ Much?", *American Economic Review*, 75: 341–351.

Schwaninger, M. (2008) *Intelligent Organizations: Powerful Models for Systemic Management*, Springer-Verlag, Berlin.

Scott Morton, F. (2000) "Why Economics has been Friutful for Strategy", *Financial Times Mastering Strategy*, 26–31, Pearson Education Ltd, London.

Stieglitz, N. and Heine, K. 2007. "Innovations and the role of complementarities in a strategic theory of the firm", *Strategic Management Journal*, 28: 1-15.

Sun, M., and E. Tse (2009) "The Resource-Based View of Competitive Advantage in Two-Sided Markets", *Journal of Management Studies*, 46(1): 45–64.

Sveiby, K. E. (1997) *The New Organizational Wealth: Managing and Measuring Knowledge Based Assets*, Berrett Koehler, San Francisco, California.

Teece, D. (2007) "Explicating Dynamics Capabilities: The Nature and Microfundations of (Sustainable) Enterprise Performance", *Strategic Management Journal*, 28: 1319–1350.

Teece, D. J., J. Pisano, and A. Shuen (1997) "Dynamic Capabilities and Strategic Management", *Strategic Management Journal*, 18: 509–533.

Thompson, A., and A. Strickland (2001) *Crafting and Executing Strategy*, McGraw-Hill, New York.

Utterback, J. M., and W. J. Abernathy (1975) "A Dynamic Model of Product and Process Innovation", *Omega*, 3(6): 639–656.

Varian, H. (2002) *Intermediate Microeconomics*, Prentice Hall, New York.

Warren, K. (2008) *Strategic Management Dynamics*, John Wiley & Sons, Hoboken, New Jersey.

Wernerfelt, B. (1984) "A Resource-Based View of the Firm", *Strategic Management Journal*, 5:171-180.

Williams, J.R. (1992) "How Sustainable is your Competitive Advantage?", *California Management Review*, 34: 29-51.

Winter, S. (2003) "Understanding Dynamic Capabilities", *Strategic Management Journal*, 24: 991–995.

Zott, C., and R. Amit (2008) "The Fit between Product Market Strategy and Business Model: Implications for Firm Performance", *Strategic Management Journal*, 29(1): 1–26.

Index